The Celestial Song
or
Bhagavad-Gita

Being a Discourse Between Arjuna,
Prince of India, and the Supreme Being
Under the Form of Krishna

Translated from the Sanskrit Text
by
Sir Edwin Arnold

SASA PUBLISHING (OPC) PRIVATE LIMITED
ANDHRA PRADESH

THE CELESTIAL SONG OF BHAGAVAD - GITA

SIR EDWIN ARNOLD

REPUBLISHED IN 2026

PUBLISHED BY

SASA PUBLISHING (OPC) PRIVATE LIMITED

8-1, NEELITHOTTI KANDRIGA

SATYAVEDU – 517588, CHITOOR DISTRICT

ANDHRAPRADESH

Tel : 9441595078

sasapublishing@outlook.com

ISBN : 978-93-48584-08-3

Contents

CHAPTER I 7
CHAPTER II 12
CHAPTER III 21
CHAPTER IV 26
CHAPTER V 32
CHAPTER VI 36
CHAPTER VII 42
CHAPTER VIII 46
CHAPTER IX 50
CHAPTER X 55
CHAPTER XI 60
CHAPTER XII 72
CHAPTER XIII 75
CHAPTER XIV 80
CHAPTER XV 84
CHAPTER XVI 88
CHAPTER XVII 92
CHAPTER XVIII 96

PREFACE

This famous and marvellous Sanskrit poem occurs as an episode of the Mahabharata, in the sixth--or "Bhishma"--Parva of the great Hindoo epic. It enjoys immense popularity and authority in India, where it is reckoned as one of the ``Five Jewels,"--pancharatnani--of Devanagiri literature. In plain but noble language it unfolds a philosophical system which remains to this day the prevailing Brahmanic belief, blending as it does the doctrines of Kapila, Patanjali, and the Vedas. So lofty are many of its declarations, so sublime its aspirations, so pure and tender its piety, that Schlegel, after his study of the poem, breaks forth into this outburst of delight and praise towards its unknown author: "Magistrorum reverentia a Brachmanis inter sanctissima pietatis officia refertur. Ergo te primum, Vates sanctissime, Numinisque hypopheta! quisquis tandem inter mortales dictus tu fueris, carminis bujus auctor,, cujus oraculis mens ad excelsa quaeque,quaeque,, aeterna atque divina, cum inenarraoih quddam delectatione rapitur-te primum, inquam, salvere jubeo, et vestigia tua semper adore." Lassen re-echoes this splendid tribute; and indeed, so striking are some of the moralities here inculcated, and so close the parallelism--ofttimes actually verbal-- between its teachings and those of the New Testament, that a controversy has arisen between Pandits and Missionaries on the point whether the author borrowed from Christian sources, or the Evangelists and Apostles from him.

This raises the question of its date, which cannot be positively settled. It must have been inlaid into the ancient epic at a period later than that of the original Mahabharata, but Mr Kasinath Telang has offered some fair arguments to prove it anterior to the Christian era. The weight of evidence, however, tends to place its composition at about the third century after Christ; and perhaps there are really echoes in this Brahmanic poem of the lessons of Galilee, and of the Syrian incarnation.

Its scene is the level country between the Jumna and the Sarsooti rivers-now Kurnul and Jheend. Its simple plot consists of a dialogue held by Prince Arjuna, the brother of King Yudhisthira, with Krishna, the Supreme Deity, wearing the disguise of a charioteer. A great battle is impending between the armies of the Kauravas and Pandavas, and this conversation is maintained in a war-chariot drawn up between the opposing hosts.

The poem has been turned into French by Burnouf, into Latin by Lassen, into Italian by Stanislav Gatti, into Greek by Galanos, and into English by Mr. Thomson and Mr Davies, the prose transcript of the last-named being truly beyond praise for its fidelity and clearness. Mr Telang has also published at Bombay a version in colloquial rhythm, eminently learned and intelligent, but not conveying the dignity or grace of the original. If I venture to offer a translation of the wonderful poem after so many superior scholars, it is in grateful recognition of the help derived from their labours, and because English literature would certainly be incomplete without possessing in popular form a poetical and philosophical work so dear to India.

There is little else to say which the "Song Celestial" does not explain for itself. The Sanskrit original is written in the Anushtubh metre, which cannot be successfully reproduced for Western ears. I have therefore cast it into our flexible blank verse, changing into lyrical measures where the text itself similarly breaks. For the most part, I believe the sense to be faithfully preserved in the following pages; but Schlegel himself had to say: "In reconditioribus me semper poetafoster mentem recte divinasse affirmare non ausim." Those who would read more upon the philosophy of the poem may find an admirable introduction in the volume of Mr Davies, printed by Messrs Trubner & Co.

EDWIN ARNOLD, C.S.I.

CHAPTER I

Dhritirashtra:
Ranged thus for battle on the sacred plain--
On Kurukshetra--say, Sanjaya! say
What wrought my people, and the Pandavas?
Sanjaya:
When he beheld the host of Pandavas,
Raja Duryodhana to Drona drew,
And spake these words: "Ah, Guru! see this line,
How vast it is of Pandu fighting-men,
Embattled by the son of Drupada,
Thy scholar in the war! Therein stand ranked
Chiefs like Arjuna, like to Bhima chiefs,
Benders of bows; Virata, Yuyudhan,
Drupada, eminent upon his car,
Dhrishtaket, Chekitan, Kasi's stout lord,
Purujit, Kuntibhoj, and Saivya,
With Yudhamanyu, and Uttamauj
Subhadra's child; and Drupadi's;-all famed!
All mounted on their shining chariots!
On our side, too,--thou best of Brahmans! see
Excellent chiefs, commanders of my line,
Whose names I joy to count: thyself the first,

Then Bhishma, Karna, Kripa fierce in fight,
Vikarna, Aswatthaman; next to these
Strong Saumadatti, with full many more
Valiant and tried, ready this day to die
For me their king, each with his weapon grasped,
Each skilful in the field. Weakest-meseems-
Our battle shows where Bhishma holds command,
And Bhima, fronting him, something too strong!
Have care our captains nigh to Bhishma's ranks
Prepare what help they may! Now, blow my shell!"
    Then, at the signal of the aged king,
With blare to wake the blood, rolling around
Like to a lion's roar, the trumpeter
Blew the great Conch; and, at the noise of it,
Trumpets and drums, cymbals and gongs and horns
Burst into sudden clamour; as the blasts
Of loosened tempest, such the tumult seemed!
Then might be seen, upon their car of gold
Yoked with white steeds, blowing their battle-shells,
Krishna the God, Arjuna at his side:
Krishna, with knotted locks, blew his great conch
Carved of the "Giant's bone;" Arjuna blew
Indra's loud gift; Bhima the terrible--
Wolf-bellied Bhima-blew a long reed-conch;
And Yudhisthira, Kunti's blameless son,
Winded a mighty shell, "Victory's Voice;"
And Nakula blew shrill upon his conch
Named the "Sweet-sounding," Sahadev on his
Called"Gem-bedecked," and Kasi's Prince on his.
Sikhandi on his car, Dhrishtadyumn,
Virata, Satyaki the Unsubdued,
Drupada, with his sons, (O Lord of Earth!)
Long-armed Subhadra's children, all blew loud,

So that the clangour shook their foemen's hearts,
With quaking earth and thundering heav'n.
Then 'twas-
Beholding Dhritirashtra's battle set,
Weapons unsheathing, bows drawn forth, the war
Instant to break-Arjun, whose ensign-badge
Was Hanuman the monkey, spake this thing
To Krishna the Divine, his charioteer:
"Drive, Dauntless One! to yonder open ground
Betwixt the armies; I would see more nigh
These who will fight with us, those we must slay
To-day, in war's arbitrament; for, sure,
On bloodshed all are bent who throng this plain,
Obeying Dhritirashtra's sinful son."
Thus, by Arjuna prayed, (O Bharata!)
Between the hosts that heavenly Charioteer
Drove the bright car, reining its milk-white steeds
Where Bhishma led,and Drona,and their Lords.
"See!" spake he to Arjuna, "where they stand,
Thy kindred of the Kurus:" and the Prince
Marked on each hand the kinsmen of his house,
Grandsires and sires, uncles and brothers and sons,
Cousins and sons-in-law and nephews, mixed
With friends and honoured elders; some this side,
Some that side ranged: and, seeing those opposed,
Such kith grown enemies-Arjuna's heart
Melted with pity, while he uttered this:
Arjuna.
Krishna! as I behold, come here to shed
Their common blood, yon concourse of our kin,
My members fail, my tongue dries in my mouth,
A shudder thrills my body, and my hair
Bristles with horror; from my weak hand slips

Gandiv, the goodly bow; a fever burns
My skin to parching; hardly may I stand;
The life within me seems to swim and faint;
Nothing do I foresee save woe and wail!
It is not good, O Keshav! nought of good
Can spring from mutual slaughter! Lo, I hate
Triumph and domination, wealth and ease,
Thus sadly won! Aho! what victory
Can bring delight, Govinda! what rich spoils
Could profit; what rule recompense; what span
Of life itself seem sweet, bought with such blood?
Seeing that these stand here, ready to die,
For whose sake life was fair, and pleasure pleased,
And power grew precious:-grandsires, sires, and sons,
Brothers, and fathers-in-law, and sons-in-law,
Elders and friends! Shall I deal death on these
Even though they seek to slay us? Not one blow,
O Madhusudan! will I strike to gain
The rule of all Three Worlds; then, how much less
To seize an earthly kingdom! Killing these
Must breed but anguish, Krishna! If they be
Guilty, we shall grow guilty by their deaths;
Their sins will light on us, if we shall slay
Those sons of Dhritirashtra, and our kin;
What peace could come of that, O Madhava?
For if indeed, blinded by lust and wrath,
These cannot see, or will not see, the sin
Of kingly lines o'erthrown and kinsmen slain,
How should not we, who see, shun such a crime--
We who perceive the guilt and feel the shame--
O thou Delight of Men, Janardana?
By overthrow of houses perisheth
Their sweet continuous household piety,

And-rites neglected, piety extinct--
Enters impiety upon that home;
Its women grow unwomaned, whence there spring
Mad passions, and the mingling-up of castes,
Sending a Hell-ward road that family,
And whoso wrought its doom by wicked wrath.
Nay, and the souls of honoured ancestors
Fall from their place of peace, being bereft
Of funeral-cakes and the wan death-water.[FN#1]
So teach our holy hymns. Thus, if we slay
Kinsfolk and friends for love of earthly power,
Ahovat! what an evil fault it were!
Better I deem it, if my kinsmen strike,
To face them weaponless, and bare my breast
To shaft and spear, than answer blow with blow.

So speaking, in the face of those two hosts,
Arjuna sank upon his chariot-seat,
And let fall bow and arrows, sick at heart.

HERE ENDETH CHAPTER I. OF THE BHAGAVAD-GITA,
Entitled "Arjun-Vishad,"
Or "The Book of the Distress of Arjuna."

CHAPTER II

Sanjaya.
Him, filled with such compassion and such grief,
With eyes tear-dimmed, despondent, in stern words
The Driver, Madhusudan, thus addressed:
Krishna.
How hath this weakness taken thee? Whence springs
The inglorious trouble, shameful to the brave,
Barring the path of virtue? Nay, Arjun!
Forbid thyself to feebleness! it mars
Thy warrior-name! cast off the coward-fit!
Wake! Be thyself! Arise, Scourge of thy Foes!
Arjuna.
How can I, in the battle, shoot with shafts
On Bhishma, or on Drona-O thou Chief!--
Both worshipful, both honourable men?
Better to live on beggar's bread
With those we love alive,
Than taste their blood in rich feasts spread,
And guiltily survive!
Ah! were it worse-who knows?--to be
Victor or vanquished here,
When those confront us angrily
Whose death leaves living drear?
In pity lost, by doubtings tossed,

My thoughts-distracted-turn
To Thee, the Guide I reverence most,
That I may counsel learn:
I know not what would heal the grief
Burned into soul and sense,
If I were earth's unchallenged chief--
A god--and these gone thence!

Sanjaya.

So spake Arjuna to the Lord of Hearts,
And sighing,"I will not fight!" held silence then.
To whom, with tender smile, (O Bharata!)
While the Prince wept despairing 'twixt those hosts,
Krishna made answer in divinest verse:

Krishna.

Thou grievest where no grief should be! thou speak'st
Words lacking wisdom! for the wise in heart
Mourn not for those that live, nor those that die.
Nor I, nor thou, nor any one of these,
Ever was not, nor ever will not be,
For ever and for ever afterwards.
All, that doth live, lives always! To man's frame
As there come infancy and youth and age,
So come there raisings-up and layings-down
Of other and of other life-abodes,
Which the wise know, and fear not. This that irks--
Thy sense-life, thrilling to the elements--
Bringing thee heat and cold, sorrows and joys,
'Tis brief and mutable! Bear with it, Prince!
As the wise bear. The soul which is not moved,
The soul that with a strong and constant calm
Takes sorrow and takes joy indifferently,
Lives in the life undying! That which is
Can never cease to be; that which is not

Will not exist. To see this truth of both
Is theirs who part essence from accident,
Substance from shadow. Indestructible,
Learn thou! the Life is, spreading life through all;
It cannot anywhere, by any means,
Be anywise diminished, stayed, or changed.
But for these fleeting frames which it informs
With spirit deathless, endless, infinite,
They perish. Let them perish, Prince! and fight!
He who shall say, "Lo! I have slain a man!"
He who shall think, "Lo! I am slain!" those both
Know naught! Life cannot slay. Life is not slain!
Never the spirit was born; the spirit shall cease to be never;
Never was time it was not; End and Beginning are dreams!
Birthless and deathless and changeless remaineth the spirit for ever;
Death hath not touched it at all, dead though the house of it seems!

Who knoweth it exhaustless, self-sustained,
Immortal, indestructible,--shall such
Say, "I have killed a man, or caused to kill?"

Nay, but as when one layeth
His worn-out robes away,
And taking new ones, sayeth,
"These will I wear to-day!"
So putteth by the spirit
Lightly its garb of flesh,
And passeth to inherit
A residence afresh.

I say to thee weapons reach not the Life;
Flame burns it not, waters cannot o'erwhelm,
Nor dry winds wither it. Impenetrable,
Unentered, unassailed, unharmed, untouched,

Immortal, all-arriving, stable, sure,
Invisible, ineffable, by word
And thought uncompassed, ever all itself,
Thus is the Soul declared! How wilt thou, then,--
Knowing it so,--grieve when thou shouldst not grieve?
How, if thou hearest that the man new-dead
Is, like the man new-born, still living man--
One same, existent Spirit--wilt thou weep?
The end of birth is death; the end of death
Is birth: this is ordained! and mournest thou,
Chief of the stalwart arm! for what befalls
Which could not otherwise befall? The birth
Of living things comes unperceived; the death
Comes unperceived; between them, beings perceive:
What is there sorrowful herein, dear Prince?
    Wonderful, wistful, to contemplate!
Difficult, doubtful, to speak upon!
Strange and great for tongue to relate,
Mystical hearing for every one!
Nor wotteth man this, what a marvel it is,
When seeing, and saying, and hearing are done!
    This Life within all living things, my Prince!
Hides beyond harm; scorn thou to suffer, then,
For that which cannot suffer. Do thy part!
Be mindful of thy name, and tremble not!
Nought better can betide a martial soul
Than lawful war; happy the warrior
To whom comes joy of battle--comes, as now,
Glorious and fair, unsought; opening for him
A gateway unto Heav'n. But, if thou shunn'st
This honourable field--a Kshattriya--
If, knowing thy duty and thy task, thou bidd'st
Duty and task go by--that shall be sin!

And those to come shall speak thee infamy
From age to age; but infamy is worse
For men of noble blood to bear than death!
The chiefs upon their battle-chariots
Will deem 'twas fear that drove thee from the fray.
Of those who held thee mighty-souled the scorn
Thou must abide, while all thine enemies
Will scatter bitter speech of thee, to mock
The valour which thou hadst; what fate could fall
More grievously than this? Either--being killed--
Thou wilt win Swarga's safety, or--alive
And victor--thou wilt reign an earthly king.
Therefore, arise, thou Son of Kunti! brace
Thine arm for conflict, nerve thy heart to meet--
As things alike to thee--pleasure or pain,
Profit or ruin, victory or defeat:
So minded, gird thee to the fight, for so
Thou shalt not sin!

Thus far I speak to thee
As from the "Sankhya"--unspiritually--
Hear now the deeper teaching of the Yog,
Which holding, understanding, thou shalt burst
Thy Karmabandh, the bondage of wrought deeds.
Here shall no end be hindered, no hope marred,
No loss be feared: faith--yea, a little faith--
Shall save thee from the anguish of thy dread.
Here, Glory of the Kurus! shines one rule--
One steadfast rule--while shifting souls have laws
Many and hard. Specious, but wrongful deem
The speech of those ill-taught ones who extol
The letter of their Vedas, saying, "This
Is all we have, or need;" being weak at heart
With wants, seekers of Heaven: which comes--they say--

As "fruit of good deeds done;" promising men
Much profit in new births for works of faith;
In various rites abounding; following whereon
Large merit shall accrue towards wealth and power;
Albeit, who wealth and power do most desire
Least fixity of soul have such, least hold
On heavenly meditation. Much these teach,
From Veds, concerning the "three qualities;"
But thou, be free of the "three qualities,"
Free of the "pairs of opposites,"[FN#2] and free
From that sad righteousness which calculates;
Self-ruled, Arjuna! simple, satisfied![FN#3]
Look! like as when a tank pours water forth
To suit all needs, so do these Brahmans draw
Text for all wants from tank of Holy Writ.
But thou, want not! ask not! Find full reward
Of doing right in right! Let right deeds be
Thy motive, not the fruit which comes from them.
And live in action! Labour! Make thine acts
Thy piety, casting all self aside,
Contemning gain and merit; equable
In good or evil: equability
Is Yog, is piety!

Yet, the right act
Is less, far less, than the right-thinking mind.
Seek refuge in thy soul; have there thy heaven!
Scorn them that follow virtue for her gifts!
The mind of pure devotion--even here--
Casts equally aside good deeds and bad,
Passing above them. Unto pure devotion
Devote thyself: with perfect meditation
Comes perfect act, and the right-hearted rise--
More certainly because they seek no gain--

Forth from the bands of body, step by step,
To highest seats of bliss. When thy firm soul
Hath shaken off those tangled oracles
Which ignorantly guide, then shall it soar
To high neglect of what's denied or said,
This way or that way, in doctrinal writ.
Troubled no longer by the priestly lore,
Safe shall it live, and sure; steadfastly bent
On meditation. This is Yog--and Peace!

Arjuna.

What is his mark who hath that steadfast heart,
Confirmed in holy meditation? How
Know we his speech, Kesava? Sits he, moves he
Like other men?

Krishna.

When one, O Pritha's Son!
Abandoning desires which shake the mind--
Finds in his soul full comfort for his soul,
He hath attained the Yog--that man is such!
In sorrows not dejected, and in joys
Not overjoyed; dwelling outside the stress
Of passion, fear, and anger; fixed in calms
Of lofty contemplation;--such an one
Is Muni, is the Sage, the true Recluse!
He who to none and nowhere overbound
By ties of flesh, takes evil things and good
Neither desponding nor exulting, such
Bears wisdom's plainest mark! He who shall draw
As the wise tortoise draws its four feet safe
Under its shield, his five frail senses back
Under the spirit's buckler from the world
Which else assails them, such an one, my Prince!
Hath wisdom's mark! Things that solicit sense

Hold off from the self-governed; nay, it comes,
The appetites of him who lives beyond
Depart,--aroused no more. Yet may it chance,
O Son of Kunti! that a governed mind
Shall some time feel the sense-storms sweep, and wrest
Strong self-control by the roots. Let him regain
His kingdom! let him conquer this, and sit
On Me intent. That man alone is wise
Who keeps the mastery of himself! If one
Ponders on objects of the sense, there springs
Attraction; from attraction grows desire,
Desire flames to fierce passion, passion breeds
Recklessness; then the memory--all betrayed--
Lets noble purpose go, and saps the mind,
Till purpose, mind, and man are all undone.
But, if one deals with objects of the sense
Not loving and not hating, making them
Serve his free soul, which rests serenely lord,
Lo! such a man comes to tranquillity;
And out of that tranquillity shall rise
The end and healing of his earthly pains,
Since the will governed sets the soul at peace.
The soul of the ungoverned is not his,
Nor hath he knowledge of himself; which lacked,
How grows serenity? and, wanting that,
Whence shall he hope for happiness?
    The mind
That gives itself to follow shows of sense
Seeth its helm of wisdom rent away,
And, like a ship in waves of whirlwind, drives
To wreck and death. Only with him, great Prince!
Whose senses are not swayed by things of sense--
Only with him who holds his mastery,

Shows wisdom perfect. What is midnight-gloom
To unenlightened souls shines wakeful day
To his clear gaze; what seems as wakeful day
Is known for night, thick night of ignorance,
To his true-seeing eyes. Such is the Saint!
    And like the ocean, day by day receiving
Floods from all lands, which never overflows
Its boundary-line not leaping, and not leaving,
Fed by the rivers, but unswelled by those;--
    So is the perfect one! to his soul's ocean
The world of sense pours streams of witchery;
They leave him as they find, without commotion,
Taking their tribute, but remaining sea.
    Yea! whoso, shaking off the yoke of flesh
Lives lord, not servant, of his lusts; set free
From pride, from passion, from the sin of "Self,"
Toucheth tranquillity! O Pritha's Son!
That is the state of Brahm! There rests no dread
When that last step is reached! Live where he will,
Die when he may, such passeth from all 'plaining,
To blest Nirvana, with the Gods, attaining.

HERE ENDETH CHAPTER II. OF THE BHAGAVAD-GITA,
Entitled "Sankhya-Yog,"
Or "The Book of Doctrines."

CHAPTER III

Arjuna.
Thou whom all mortals praise, Janardana!
If meditation be a nobler thing
Than action, wherefore, then, great Kesava!
Dost thou impel me to this dreadful fight?
Now am I by thy doubtful speech disturbed!
Tell me one thing, and tell me certainly;
By what road shall I find the better end?
Krishna.
I told thee, blameless Lord! there be two paths
Shown to this world; two schools of wisdom.
First
The Sankhya's, which doth save in way of works
Prescribed[FN#4] by reason; next, the Yog, which bids
Attain by meditation, spiritually:
Yet these are one! No man shall 'scape from act
By shunning action; nay, and none shall come
By mere renouncements unto perfectness.
Nay, and no jot of time, at any time,
Rests any actionless; his nature's law
Compels him, even unwilling, into act;
[For thought is act in fancy]. He who sits
Suppressing all the instruments of flesh,
Yet in his idle heart thinking on them,

Plays the inept and guilty hypocrite:
But he who, with strong body serving mind,
Gives up his mortal powers to worthy work,
Not seeking gain, Arjuna! such an one
Is honourable. Do thine allotted task!
Work is more excellent than idleness;
The body's life proceeds not, lacking work.
There is a task of holiness to do,
Unlike world-binding toil, which bindeth not
The faithful soul; such earthly duty do
Free from desire, and thou shalt well perform
Thy heavenly purpose. Spake Prajapati--
In the beginning, when all men were made,
And, with mankind, the sacrifice-- "Do this!
Work! sacrifice! Increase and multiply
With sacrifice! This shall be Kamaduk,
Your 'Cow of Plenty,' giving back her milk
Of all abundance. Worship the gods thereby;
The gods shall yield thee grace. Those meats ye crave
The gods will grant to Labour, when it pays
Tithes in the altar-flame. But if one eats
Fruits of the earth, rendering to kindly Heaven
No gift of toil, that thief steals from his world."
Who eat of food after their sacrifice
Are quit of fault, but they that spread a feast
All for themselves, eat sin and drink of sin.
By food the living live; food comes of rain,
And rain comes by the pious sacrifice,
And sacrifice is paid with tithes of toil;
Thus action is of Brahma, who is One,
The Only, All-pervading; at all times
Present in sacrifice. He that abstains
To help the rolling wheels of this great world,

Glutting his idle sense, lives a lost life,
Shameful and vain. Existing for himself,
Self-concentrated, serving self alone,
No part hath he in aught; nothing achieved,
Nought wrought or unwrought toucheth him; no hope
Of help for all the living things of earth
Depends from him.[FN#5] Therefore, thy task prescribed
With spirit unattached gladly perform,
Since in performance of plain duty man
Mounts to his highest bliss. By works alone
Janak and ancient saints reached blessedness!
Moreover, for the upholding of thy kind,
Action thou should'st embrace. What the wise choose
The unwise people take; what best men do
The multitude will follow. Look on me,
Thou Son of Pritha! in the three wide worlds
I am not bound to any toil, no height
Awaits to scale, no gift remains to gain,
Yet I act here! and, if I acted not--
Earnest and watchful--those that look to me
For guidance, sinking back to sloth again
Because I slumbered, would decline from good,
And I should break earth's order and commit
Her offspring unto ruin, Bharata!
Even as the unknowing toil, wedded to sense,
So let the enlightened toil, sense-freed, but set
To bring the world deliverance, and its bliss;
Not sowing in those simple, busy hearts
Seed of despair. Yea! let each play his part
In all he finds to do, with unyoked soul.
All things are everywhere by Nature wrought
In interaction of the qualities.
The fool, cheated by self, thinks, "This I did"

And "That I wrought; "but--ah, thou strong-armed Prince!--
A better-lessoned mind, knowing the play
Of visible things within the world of sense,
And how the qualities must qualify,
Standeth aloof even from his acts. Th' untaught
Live mixed with them, knowing not Nature's way,
Of highest aims unwitting, slow and dull.
Those make thou not to stumble, having the light;
But all thy dues discharging, for My sake,
With meditation centred inwardly,
Seeking no profit, satisfied, serene,
Heedless of issue--fight! They who shall keep
My ordinance thus, the wise and willing hearts,
Have quittance from all issue of their acts;
But those who disregard My ordinance,
Thinking they know, know nought, and fall to loss,
Confused and foolish. 'Sooth, the instructed one
Doth of his kind, following what fits him most:
And lower creatures of their kind; in vain
Contending 'gainst the law. Needs must it be
The objects of the sense will stir the sense
To like and dislike, yet th' enlightened man
Yields not to these, knowing them enemies.
Finally, this is better, that one do
His own task as he may, even though he fail,
Than take tasks not his own, though they seem good.
To die performing duty is no ill;
But who seeks other roads shall wander still.

Arjuna.

Yet tell me, Teacher! by what force doth man
Go to his ill, unwilling; as if one
Pushed him that evil path?

Krishna.

Kama it is!
Passion it is! born of the Darknesses,
Which pusheth him. Mighty of appetite,
Sinful, and strong is this!--man's enemy!
As smoke blots the white fire, as clinging rust
Mars the bright mirror, as the womb surrounds
The babe unborn, so is the world of things
Foiled, soiled, enclosed in this desire of flesh.
The wise fall, caught in it; the unresting foe
It is of wisdom, wearing countless forms,
Fair but deceitful, subtle as a flame.
Sense, mind, and reason--these, O Kunti's Son!
Are booty for it; in its play with these
It maddens man, beguiling, blinding him.
Therefore, thou noblest child of Bharata!
Govern thy heart! Constrain th' entangled sense!
Resist the false, soft sinfulness which saps
Knowledge and judgment! Yea, the world is strong,
But what discerns it stronger, and the mind
Strongest; and high o'er all the ruling Soul.
Wherefore, perceiving Him who reigns supreme,
Put forth full force of Soul in thy own soul!
Fight! vanquish foes and doubts, dear Hero! slay
What haunts thee in fond shapes, and would betray!

HERE ENDETH CHAPTER III. OF THE BHAGAVAD-GITA,

Entitled "Karma-Yog,"
Or "The Book of Virtue in Work."

CHAPTER IV

Krishna.

This deathless Yoga, this deep union,
I taught Vivaswata,[FN#6] the Lord of Light;
Vivaswata to Manu gave it; he
To Ikshwaku; so passed it down the line
Of all my royal Rishis. Then, with years,
The truth grew dim and perished, noble Prince!
Now once again to thee it is declared--
This ancient lore, this mystery supreme--
Seeing I find thee votary and friend.

Arjuna.

Thy birth, dear Lord, was in these later days,
And bright Vivaswata's preceded time!
How shall I comprehend this thing thou sayest,
"From the beginning it was I who taught?"

Krishna.

Manifold the renewals of my birth
Have been, Arjuna! and of thy births, too!
But mine I know, and thine thou knowest not,
O Slayer of thy Foes! Albeit I be
Unborn, undying, indestructible,
The Lord of all things living; not the less--
By Maya, by my magic which I stamp

On floating Nature-forms, the primal vast--
I come, and go, and come. When Righteousness
Declines, O Bharata! when Wickedness
Is strong, I rise, from age to age, and take
Visible shape, and move a man with men,
Succouring the good, thrusting the evil back,
And setting Virtue on her seat again.
Who knows the truth touching my births on earth
And my divine work, when he quits the flesh
Puts on its load no more, falls no more down
To earthly birth: to Me he comes, dear Prince!
Many there be who come! from fear set free,
From anger, from desire; keeping their hearts
Fixed upon me--my Faithful--purified
By sacred flame of Knowledge. Such as these
Mix with my being. Whoso worship me,
Them I exalt; but all men everywhere
Shall fall into my path; albeit, those souls
Which seek reward for works, make sacrifice
Now, to the lower gods. I say to thee
Here have they their reward. But I am He
Made the Four Castes, and portioned them a place
After their qualities and gifts. Yea, I
Created, the Reposeful; I that live
Immortally, made all those mortal births:
For works soil not my essence, being works
Wrought uninvolved.[FN#7] Who knows me acting thus
Unchained by action, action binds not him;
And, so perceiving, all those saints of old
Worked, seeking for deliverance. Work thou
As, in the days gone by, thy fathers did.

Thou sayst, perplexed, It hath been asked before
By singers and by sages, "What is act,

And what inaction? "I will teach thee this,
And, knowing, thou shalt learn which work doth save
Needs must one rightly meditate those three--
Doing,--not doing,--and undoing. Here
Thorny and dark the path is! He who sees
How action may be rest, rest action--he
Is wisest 'mid his kind; he hath the truth!
He doeth well, acting or resting. Freed
In all his works from prickings of desire,
Burned clean in act by the white fire of truth,
The wise call that man wise; and such an one,
Renouncing fruit of deeds, always content.
Always self-satisfying, if he works,
Doth nothing that shall stain his separate soul,
Which--quit of fear and hope--subduing self--
Rejecting outward impulse--yielding up
To body's need nothing save body, dwells
Sinless amid all sin, with equal calm
Taking what may befall, by grief unmoved,
Unmoved by joy, unenvyingly; the same
In good and evil fortunes; nowise bound
By bond of deeds. Nay, but of such an one,
Whose crave is gone, whose soul is liberate,
Whose heart is set on truth--of such an one
What work he does is work of sacrifice,
Which passeth purely into ash and smoke
Consumed upon the altar! All's then God!
The sacrifice is Brahm, the ghee and grain
Are Brahm, the fire is Brahm, the flesh it eats
Is Brahm, and unto Brahm attaineth he
Who, in such office, meditates on Brahm.
Some votaries there be who serve the gods
With flesh and altar-smoke; but other some

Who, lighting subtler fires, make purer rite
With will of worship. Of the which be they
Who, in white flame of continence, consume
Joys of the sense, delights of eye and ear,
Forgoing tender speech and sound of song:
And they who, kindling fires with torch of Truth,
Burn on a hidden altar-stone the bliss
Of youth and love, renouncing happiness:
And they who lay for offering there their wealth,
Their penance, meditation, piety,
Their steadfast reading of the scrolls, their lore
Painfully gained with long austerities:
And they who, making silent sacrifice,
Draw in their breath to feed the flame of thought,
And breathe it forth to waft the heart on high,
Governing the ventage of each entering air
Lest one sigh pass which helpeth not the soul:
And they who, day by day denying needs,
Lay life itself upon the altar-flame,
Burning the body wan. Lo! all these keep
The rite of offering, as if they slew
Victims; and all thereby efface much sin.
Yea! and who feed on the immortal food
Left of such sacrifice, to Brahma pass,
To The Unending. But for him that makes
No sacrifice, he hath nor part nor lot
Even in the present world. How should he share
Another, O thou Glory of thy Line?

In sight of Brahma all these offerings
Are spread and are accepted! Comprehend
That all proceed by act; for knowing this,
Thou shalt be quit of doubt. The sacrifice
Which Knowledge pays is better than great gifts

Offered by wealth, since gifts' worth--O my Prince!
Lies in the mind which gives, the will that serves:
And these are gained by reverence, by strong search,
By humble heed of those who see the Truth
And teach it. Knowing Truth, thy heart no more
Will ache with error, for the Truth shall show
All things subdued to thee, as thou to Me.
Moreover, Son of Pandu! wert thou worst
Of all wrong-doers, this fair ship of Truth
Should bear thee safe and dry across the sea
Of thy transgressions. As the kindled flame
Feeds on the fuel till it sinks to ash,
So unto ash, Arjuna! unto nought
The flame of Knowledge wastes works' dross away!
There is no purifier like thereto
In all this world, and he who seeketh it
Shall find it--being grown perfect--in himself.
Believing, he receives it when the soul
Masters itself, and cleaves to Truth, and comes--
Possessing knowledge–to the higher peace,
The uttermost repose. But those untaught,
And those without full faith, and those who fear
Are shent; no peace is here or other where,
No hope, nor happiness for whoso doubts.
He that, being self-contained, hath vanquished doubt,
Disparting self from service, soul from works,
Enlightened and emancipate, my Prince!
Works fetter him no more! Cut then atwain
With sword of wisdom, Son of Bharata!
This doubt that binds thy heart-beats! cleave the bond
Born of thy ignorance! Be bold and wise!
Give thyself to the field with me! Arise!

HERE ENDETH CHAPTER IV. OF THE BHAGAVAD-GITA,
Entitled "Jnana Yog,"
Or "The Book of the Religion of Knowledge,"

CHAPTER V

Arjuna.

Yet, Krishna! at the one time thou dost laud
Surcease of works, and, at another time,
Service through work. Of these twain plainly tell
Which is the better way?

Krishna.

To cease from works
Is well, and to do works in holiness
Is well; and both conduct to bliss supreme;
But of these twain the better way is his
Who working piously refraineth not.

That is the true Renouncer, firm and fixed,
Who--seeking nought, rejecting nought--dwells proof
Against the "opposites."[FN#8] O valiant Prince!
In doing, such breaks lightly from all deed:
'Tis the new scholar talks as they were two,
This Sankhya and this Yoga: wise men know
Who husbands one plucks golden fruit of both!
The region of high rest which Sankhyans reach
Yogins attain. Who sees these twain as one
Sees with clear eyes! Yet such abstraction, Chief!
Is hard to win without much holiness.
Whoso is fixed in holiness, self-ruled,
Pure-hearted, lord of senses and of self,

Lost in the common life of all which lives--
A "Yogayukt"--he is a Saint who wends
Straightway to Brahm. Such an one is not touched
By taint of deeds. "Nought of myself I do!"
Thus will he think-who holds the truth of truths--
In seeing, hearing, touching, smelling; when
He eats, or goes, or breathes; slumbers or talks,
Holds fast or loosens, opes his eyes or shuts;
Always assured "This is the sense-world plays
With senses."He that acts in thought of Brahm,
Detaching end from act, with act content,
The world of sense can no more stain his soul
Than waters mar th' enamelled lotus-leaf.
With life, with heart, with mind,-nay, with the help
Of all five senses--letting selfhood go--
Yogins toil ever towards their souls' release.
Such votaries, renouncing fruit of deeds,
Gain endless peace: the unvowed, the passion-bound,
Seeking a fruit from works, are fastened down.
The embodied sage, withdrawn within his soul,
At every act sits godlike in "the town
Which hath nine gateways,"[FN#9] neither doing aught
Nor causing any deed. This world's Lord makes
Neither the work, nor passion for the work,
Nor lust for fruit of work; the man's own self
Pushes to these! The Master of this World
Takes on himself the good or evil deeds
Of no man--dwelling beyond! Mankind errs here
By folly, darkening knowledge. But, for whom
That darkness of the soul is chased by light,
Splendid and clear shines manifest the Truth
As if a Sun of Wisdom sprang to shed
Its beams of dawn. Him meditating still,

Him seeking, with Him blended, stayed on Him,
The souls illuminated take that road
Which hath no turning back--their sins flung off
By strength of faith. [Who will may have this Light;
Who hath it sees.] To him who wisely sees,
The Brahman with his scrolls and sanctities,
The cow, the elephant, the unclean dog,
The Outcast gorging dog's meat, are all one.
The world is overcome--aye! even here!
By such as fix their faith on Unity.
The sinless Brahma dwells in Unity,
And they in Brahma. Be not over-glad
Attaining joy, and be not over-sad
Encountering grief, but, stayed on Brahma, still
Constant let each abide! The sage whose soul
Holds off from outer contacts, in himself
Finds bliss; to Brahma joined by piety,
His spirit tastes eternal peace. The joys
Springing from sense-life are but quickening wombs
Which breed sure griefs: those joys begin and end!
The wise mind takes no pleasure, Kunti's Son!
In such as those! But if a man shall learn,
Even while he lives and bears his body's chain,
To master lust and anger, he is blest!
He is the Yukta; he hath happiness,
Contentment, light, within: his life is merged
In Brahma's life; he doth Nirvana touch!
Thus go the Rishis unto rest, who dwell
With sins effaced, with doubts at end, with hearts
Governed and calm. Glad in all good they live,
Nigh to the peace of God; and all those live
Who pass their days exempt from greed and wrath,
Subduing self and senses, knowing the Soul!

The Saint who shuts outside his placid soul
All touch of sense, letting no contact through;
Whose quiet eyes gaze straight from fixed brows,
Whose outward breath and inward breath are drawn
Equal and slow through nostrils still and close;
That one-with organs, heart, and mind constrained,
Bent on deliverance, having put away
Passion, and fear, and rage;--hath, even now,
Obtained deliverance, ever and ever freed.
Yea! for he knows Me Who am He that heeds
The sacrifice and worship, God revealed;
And He who heeds not, being Lord of Worlds,
Lover of all that lives, God unrevealed,
Wherein who will shall find surety and shield!

HERE ENDS CHAPTER V. OF THE BHAGAVAD-GITA,
Entitled "Karmasanyasayog,"
Or "The Book of Religion by Renouncing Fruit of Works."

CHAPTER VI

Krishna.
Therefore, who doeth work rightful to do,
Not seeking gain from work, that man, O Prince!
Is Sanyasi and Yogi--both in one
And he is neither who lights not the flame
Of sacrifice, nor setteth hand to task.
Regard as true Renouncer him that makes
Worship by work, for who renounceth not
Works not as Yogin. So is that well said:
"By works the votary doth rise to faith,
And saintship is the ceasing from all works;
Because the perfect Yogin acts--but acts
Unmoved by passions and unbound by deeds,
Setting result aside.
Let each man raise
The Self by Soul, not trample down his Self,
Since Soul that is Self's friend may grow Self's foe.
Soul is Self's friend when Self doth rule o'er Self,
But Self turns enemy if Soul's own self
Hates Self as not itself.[FN#10]
The sovereign soul
Of him who lives self-governed and at peace
Is centred in itself, taking alike

Pleasure and pain; heat, cold; glory and shame.
He is the Yogi, he is Yukta, glad
With joy of light and truth; dwelling apart
Upon a peak, with senses subjugate
Whereto the clod, the rock, the glistering gold
Show all as one. By this sign is he known
Being of equal grace to comrades, friends,
Chance-comers, strangers, lovers, enemies,
Aliens and kinsmen; loving all alike,
Evil or good.

Sequestered should he sit,
Steadfastly meditating, solitary,
His thoughts controlled, his passions laid away,
Quit of belongings. In a fair, still spot
Having his fixed abode,--not too much raised,
Nor yet too low,--let him abide, his goods
A cloth, a deerskin, and the Kusa-grass.
There, setting hard his mind upon The One,
Restraining heart and senses, silent, calm,
Let him accomplish Yoga, and achieve
Pureness of soul, holding immovable
Body and neck and head, his gaze absorbed
Upon his nose-end,[FN#11] rapt from all around,
Tranquil in spirit, free of fear, intent
Upon his Brahmacharya vow, devout,
Musing on Me, lost in the thought of Me.
That Yojin, so devoted, so controlled,
Comes to the peace beyond,--My peace, the peace
Of high Nirvana!

But for earthly needs
Religion is not his who too much fasts
Or too much feasts, nor his who sleeps away
An idle mind; nor his who wears to waste

His strength in vigils. Nay, Arjuna! call
That the true piety which most removes
Earth-aches and ills, where one is moderate
In eating and in resting, and in sport;
Measured in wish and act; sleeping betimes,
Waking betimes for duty.
    When the man,
So living, centres on his soul the thought
Straitly restrained--untouched internally
By stress of sense--then is he Yukta. See!
Steadfast a lamp burns sheltered from the wind;
Such is the likeness of the Yogi's mind
Shut from sense-storms and burning bright to Heaven.
When mind broods placid, soothed with holy wont;
When Self contemplates self, and in itself
Hath comfort; when it knows the nameless joy
Beyond all scope of sense, revealed to soul--
Only to soul! and, knowing, wavers not,
True to the farther Truth; when, holding this,
It deems no other treasure comparable,
But, harboured there, cannot be stirred or shook
By any gravest grief, call that state "peace,"
That happy severance Yoga; call that man
The perfect Yogin!
    Steadfastly the will
Must toil thereto, till efforts end in ease,
And thought has passed from thinking. Shaking off
All longings bred by dreams of fame and gain,
Shutting the doorways of the senses close
With watchful ward; so, step by step, it comes
To gift of peace assured and heart assuaged,
When the mind dwells self-wrapped, and the soul broods
Cumberless. But, as often as the heart

Breaks--wild and wavering--from control, so oft
Let him re-curb it, let him rein it back
To the soul's governance; for perfect bliss
Grows only in the bosom tranquillised,
The spirit passionless, purged from offence,
Vowed to the Infinite. He who thus vows
His soul to the Supreme Soul, quitting sin,
Passes unhindered to the endless bliss
Of unity with Brahma. He so vowed,
So blended, sees the Life-Soul resident
In all things living, and all living things
In that Life-Soul contained. And whoso thus
Discerneth Me in all, and all in Me,
I never let him go; nor looseneth he
Hold upon Me; but, dwell he where he may,
Whate'er his life, in Me he dwells and lives,
Because he knows and worships Me, Who dwell
In all which lives, and cleaves to Me in all.
Arjuna! if a man sees everywhere--
Taught by his own similitude--one Life,
One Essence in the Evil and the Good,
Hold him a Yogi, yea! well-perfected!

Arjuna.

Slayer of Madhu! yet again, this Yog,
This Peace, derived from equanimity,
Made known by thee--I see no fixity
Therein, no rest, because the heart of men
Is unfixed, Krishna! rash, tumultuous,
Wilful and strong. It were all one, I think,
To hold the wayward wind, as tame man's heart.

Krishna.

Hero long-armed! beyond denial, hard
Man's heart is to restrain, and wavering;

Yet may it grow restrained by habit, Prince!
By wont of self-command. This Yog, I say,
Cometh not lightly to th' ungoverned ones;
But he who will be master of himself
Shall win it, if he stoutly strive thereto.

Arjuna.

And what road goeth he who, having faith,
Fails, Krishna! in the striving; falling back
From holiness, missing the perfect rule?
Is he not lost, straying from Brahma's light,
Like the vain cloud, which floats 'twixt earth and heaven
When lightning splits it, and it vanisheth?
Fain would I hear thee answer me herein,
Since, Krishna! none save thou can clear the doubt.

Krishna.

He is not lost, thou Son of Pritha! No!
Nor earth, nor heaven is forfeit, even for him,
Because no heart that holds one right desire
Treadeth the road of loss! He who should fail,
Desiring righteousness, cometh at death
Unto the Region of the Just; dwells there
Measureless years, and being born anew,
Beginneth life again in some fair home
Amid the mild and happy. It may chance
He doth descend into a Yogin house
On Virtue's breast; but that is rare! Such birth
Is hard to be obtained on this earth, Chief!
So hath he back again what heights of heart
He did achieve, and so he strives anew
To perfectness, with better hope, dear Prince!
For by the old desire he is drawn on
Unwittingly; and only to desire
The purity of Yog is to pass

Beyond the Sabdabrahm, the spoken Ved.
But, being Yogi, striving strong and long,
Purged from transgressions, perfected by births
Following on births, he plants his feet at last
Upon the farther path. Such as one ranks
Above ascetics, higher than the wise,
Beyond achievers of vast deeds! Be thou
Yogi Arjuna! And of such believe,
Truest and best is he who worships Me
With inmost soul, stayed on My Mystery!

HERE ENDETH CHAPTER VI. OF THE BHAGAVAD-GITA,
Entitled "Atmasanyamayog,"
Or "The Book of Religion by Self-Restraint."

CHAPTER VII

Krishna.

Learn now, dear Prince! how, if thy soul be set
Ever on Me--still exercising Yog,
Still making Me thy Refuge--thou shalt come
Most surely unto perfect hold of Me.
I will declare to thee that utmost lore,
Whole and particular, which, when thou knowest,
Leaveth no more to know here in this world.

Of many thousand mortals, one, perchance,
Striveth for Truth; and of those few that strive--
Nay, and rise high--one only--here and there--
Knoweth Me, as I am, the very Truth.

Earth, water, flame, air, ether, life, and mind,
And individuality--those eight
Make up the showing of Me, Manifest.

These be my lower Nature; learn the higher,
Whereby, thou Valiant One! this Universe
Is, by its principle of life, produced;
Whereby the worlds of visible things are born
As from a Yoni. Know! I am that womb:
I make and I unmake this Universe:
Than me there is no other Master, Prince!
No other Maker! All these hang on me

As hangs a row of pearls upon its string.
I am the fresh taste of the water; I
The silver of the moon, the gold o' the sun,
The word of worship in the Veds, the thrill
That passeth in the ether, and the strength
Of man's shed seed. I am the good sweet smell
Of the moistened earth, I am the fire's red light,
The vital air moving in all which moves,
The holiness of hallowed souls, the root
Undying, whence hath sprung whatever is;
The wisdom of the wise, the intellect
Of the informed, the greatness of the great.
The splendour of the splendid. Kunti's Son!
These am I, free from passion and desire;
Yet am I right desire in all who yearn,
Chief of the Bharatas! for all those moods,
Soothfast, or passionate, or ignorant,
Which Nature frames, deduce from me; but all
Are merged in me--not I in them! The world--
Deceived by those three qualities of being--
Wotteth not Me Who am outside them all,
Above them all, Eternal! Hard it is
To pierce that veil divine of various shows
Which hideth Me; yet they who worship Me
Pierce it and pass beyond.

I am not known
To evil-doers, nor to foolish ones,
Nor to the base and churlish; nor to those
Whose mind is cheated by the show of things,
Nor those that take the way of Asuras.[FN#12]

Four sorts of mortals know me: he who weeps,
Arjuna! and the man who yearns to know;

And he who toils to help; and he who sits
Certain of me, enlightened.
Of these four,
O Prince of India! highest, nearest, best
That last is, the devout soul, wise, intent
Upon "The One." Dear, above all, am I
To him; and he is dearest unto me!
All four are good, and seek me; but mine own,
The true of heart, the faithful--stayed on me,
Taking me as their utmost blessedness,
They are not "mine,"but I--even I myself!
At end of many births to Me they come!
Yet hard the wise Mahatma is to find,
That man who sayeth, "All is Vasudev!"[FN#13]
There be those, too, whose knowledge, turned aside
By this desire or that, gives them to serve
Some lower gods, with various rites, constrained
By that which mouldeth them. Unto all such--
Worship what shrine they will, what shapes, in faith--
'Tis I who give them faith! I am content!
The heart thus asking favour from its God,
Darkened but ardent, hath the end it craves,
The lesser blessing--but 'tis I who give!
Yet soon is withered what small fruit they reap:
Those men of little minds, who worship so,
Go where they worship, passing with their gods.
But Mine come unto me! Blind are the eyes
Which deem th' Unmanifested manifest,
Not comprehending Me in my true Self!
Imperishable, viewless, undeclared,
Hidden behind my magic veil of shows,
I am not seen by all; I am not known--
Unborn and changeless--to the idle world.

But I, Arjuna! know all things which were,
And all which are, and all which are to be,
Albeit not one among them knoweth Me!

By passion for the "pairs of opposites,"
By those twain snares of Like and Dislike, Prince!
All creatures live bewildered, save some few
Who, quit of sins, holy in act, informed,
Freed from the "opposites,"and fixed in faith,
Cleave unto Me.

Who cleave, who seek in Me
Refuge from birth[FN#14] and death, those have the Truth!
Those know Me BRAHMA; know Me Soul of Souls,
The ADHYATMAN; know KARMA, my work;
Know I am ADHIBHUTA, Lord of Life,
And ADHIDAIVA, Lord of all the Gods,
And ADHIYAJNA, Lord of Sacrifice;
Worship Me well, with hearts of love and faith,
And find and hold me in the hour of death.

HERE ENDETH CHAPTER VII. OF THE BHAGAVAD-GITA,
Entitled "Vijnanayog,"
Or "The Book of Religion by Discernment."

CHAPTER VIII

Arjuna.
Who is that BRAHMA? What that Soul of Souls,
The ADHYATMAN? What, Thou Best of All!
Thy work, the KARMA? Tell me what it is
Thou namest ADHIBHUTA? What again
Means ADHIDAIVA? Yea, and how it comes
Thou canst be ADHIYAJNA in thy flesh?
Slayer of Madhu! Further, make me know
How good men find thee in the hour of death?

Krishna.
I BRAHMA am! the One Eternal GOD,
And ADHYATMAN is My Being's name,
The Soul of Souls! What goeth forth from Me,
Causing all life to live, is KARMA called:
And, Manifested in divided forms,
I am the ADHIBHUTA, Lord of Lives;
And ADHIDAIVA, Lord of all the Gods,
Because I am PURUSHA, who begets.
And ADHIYAJNA, Lord of Sacrifice,
I--speaking with thee in this body here--
Am, thou embodied one! (for all the shrines
Flame unto Me!) And, at the hour of death,
He that hath meditated Me alone,
In putting off his flesh, comes forth to Me,

Enters into My Being--doubt thou not!
But, if he meditated otherwise
At hour of death, in putting off the flesh,
He goes to what he looked for, Kunti's Son!
Because the Soul is fashioned to its like.

Have Me, then, in thy heart always! and fight!
Thou too, when heart and mind are fixed on Me,
Shalt surely come to Me! All come who cleave
With never-wavering will of firmest faith,
Owning none other Gods: all come to Me,
The Uttermost, Purusha, Holiest!

Whoso hath known Me, Lord of sage and singer,
Ancient of days; of all the Three Worlds Stay,
Boundless,--but unto every atom Bringer
Of that which quickens it: whoso, I say,

Hath known My form, which passeth mortal knowing;
Seen my effulgence--which no eye hath seen--
Than the sun's burning gold more brightly glowing,
Dispersing darkness,--unto him hath been

Right life! And, in the hour when life is ending,
With mind set fast and trustful piety,
Drawing still breath beneath calm brows unbending,
In happy peace that faithful one doth die,--

In glad peace passeth to Purusha's heaven.
The place which they who read the Vedas name
AKSHARAM, "Ultimate;" whereto have striven
Saints and ascetics--their road is the same.

That way--the highest way--goes he who shuts
The gates of all his senses, locks desire
Safe in his heart, centres the vital airs
Upon his parting thought, steadfastly set;
And, murmuring OM, the sacred syllable--
Emblem of BRAHM--dies, meditating Me.

For who, none other Gods regarding, looks
Ever to Me, easily am I gained
By such a Yogi; and, attaining Me,
They fall not--those Mahatmas--back to birth,
To life, which is the place of pain, which ends,
But take the way of utmost blessedness.

The worlds, Arjuna!--even Brahma's world--
Roll back again from Death to Life's unrest;
But they, O Kunti's Son! that reach to Me,
Taste birth no more. If ye know Brahma's Day
Which is a thousand Yugas; if ye know
The thousand Yugas making Brahma's Night,
Then know ye Day and Night as He doth know!
When that vast Dawn doth break, th' Invisible
Is brought anew into the Visible;
When that deep Night doth darken, all which is
Fades back again to Him Who sent it forth;
Yea! this vast company of living things--
Again and yet again produced--expires
At Brahma's Nightfall; and, at Brahma's Dawn,
Riseth, without its will, to life new-born.
But--higher, deeper, innermost--abides
Another Life, not like the life of sense,
Escaping sight, unchanging. This endures
When all created things have passed away:
This is that Life named the Unmanifest,
The Infinite! the All! the Uttermost.
Thither arriving none return. That Life
Is Mine, and I am there! And, Prince! by faith
Which wanders not, there is a way to come
Thither. I, the PURUSHA, I Who spread
The Universe around me--in Whom dwell
All living Things--may so be reached and seen!

. . . . [FN#14]

Richer than holy fruit on Vedas growing,
Greater than gifts, better than prayer or fast,
Such wisdom is! The Yogi, this way knowing,
Comes to the Utmost Perfect Peace at last.

HERE ENDETH CHAPTER VIII. OF THE BHAGAVAD-GITA,

Entitled "Aksharaparabrahmayog,"

Or "The book of Religion by Devotion to the One Supreme God."

CHAPTER IX

Krishna.

Now will I open unto thee--whose heart
Rejects not--that last lore, deepest-concealed,
That farthest secret of My Heavens and Earths,
Which but to know shall set thee free from ills,--
A royal lore! a Kingly mystery!
Yea! for the soul such light as purgeth it
From every sin; a light of holiness
With inmost splendour shining; plain to see;
Easy to walk by, inexhaustible!

They that receive not this, failing in faith
To grasp the greater wisdom, reach not Me,
Destroyer of thy foes! They sink anew
Into the realm of Flesh, where all things change!

By Me the whole vast Universe of things
Is spread abroad;--by Me, the Unmanifest!
In Me are all existences contained;
Not I in them!

Yet they are not contained,
Those visible things! Receive and strive to embrace
The mystery majestical! My Being--

Creating all, sustaining all--still dwells
Outside of all!

See! as the shoreless airs
Move in the measureless space, but are not space,
[And space were space without the moving airs];
So all things are in Me, but are not I.

At closing of each Kalpa, Indian Prince!
All things which be back to My Being come:
At the beginning of each Kalpa, all
Issue new-born from Me.

By Energy
And help of Prakriti my outer Self,
Again, and yet again, I make go forth
The realms of visible things--without their will--
All of them--by the power of Prakriti.

Yet these great makings, Prince! involve Me not
Enchain Me not! I sit apart from them,
Other, and Higher, and Free; nowise attached!

Thus doth the stuff of worlds, moulded by Me,
Bring forth all that which is, moving or still,
Living or lifeless! Thus the worlds go on!

The minds untaught mistake Me, veiled in form;--
Naught see they of My secret Presence, nought
Of My hid Nature, ruling all which lives.
Vain hopes pursuing, vain deeds doing; fed
On vainest knowledge, senselessly they seek
An evil way, the way of brutes and fiends.
But My Mahatmas, those of noble soul
Who tread the path celestial, worship Me
With hearts unwandering,--knowing Me the Source,
Th' Eternal Source, of Life. Unendingly
They glorify Me; seek Me; keep their vows
Of reverence and love, with changeless faith

Adoring Me. Yea, and those too adore,
Who, offering sacrifice of wakened hearts,
Have sense of one pervading Spirit's stress,
One Force in every place, though manifold!
I am the Sacrifice! I am the Prayer!
I am the Funeral-Cake set for the dead!
I am the healing herb! I am the ghee,
The Mantra, and the flame, and that which burns!
I am-of all this boundless Universe-
The Father, Mother, Ancestor, and Guard!
The end of Learning! That which purifies
In lustral water! I am OM! I am
Rig-Veda, Sama-Veda, Yajur-Ved;
The Way, the Fosterer, the Lord, the Judge,
The Witness; the Abode, the Refuge-House,
The Friend, the Fountain and the Sea of Life
Which sends, and swallows up; Treasure of Worlds
And Treasure-Chamber! Seed and Seed-Sower,
Whence endless harvests spring! Sun's heat is mine;
Heaven's rain is mine to grant or to withhold;
Death am I, and Immortal Life I am,
Arjuna! SAT and ASAT, Visible Life,
And Life Invisible!

Yea! those who learn
The threefold Veds, who drink the Soma-wine,
Purge sins, pay sacrifice--from Me they earn
Passage to Swarga; where the meats divine
Of great gods feed them in high Indra's heaven.
Yet they, when that prodigious joy is o'er,
Paradise spent, and wage for merits given,
Come to the world of death and change once more.

They had their recompense! they stored their treasure,
Following the threefold Scripture and its writ;

Who seeketh such gaineth the fleeting pleasure
Of joy which comes and goes! I grant them it!
    But to those blessed ones who worship Me,
Turning not otherwhere, with minds set fast,
I bring assurance of full bliss beyond.
    Nay, and of hearts which follow other gods
In simple faith, their prayers arise to me,
O Kunti's Son! though they pray wrongfully;
For I am the Receiver and the Lord
Of every sacrifice, which these know not
Rightfully; so they fall to earth again!
Who follow gods go to their gods; who vow
Their souls to Pitris go to Pitris; minds
To evil Bhuts given o'er sink to the Bhuts;
And whoso loveth Me cometh to Me.
Whoso shall offer Me in faith and love
A leaf, a flower, a fruit, water poured forth,
That offering I accept, lovingly made
With pious will. Whate'er thou doest, Prince!
Eating or sacrificing, giving gifts,
Praying or fasting, let it all be done
For Me, as Mine. So shalt thou free thyself
From Karmabandh, the chain which holdeth men
To good and evil issue, so shalt come
Safe unto Me-when thou art quit of flesh--
By faith and abdication joined to Me!
    I am alike for all! I know not hate,
I know not favour! What is made is Mine!
But them that worship Me with love, I love;
They are in Me, and I in them!
    Nay, Prince!
If one of evil life turn in his thought
Straightly to Me, count him amidst the good;

He hath the high way chosen; he shall grow
Righteous ere long; he shall attain that peace
Which changes not. Thou Prince of India!
Be certain none can perish, trusting Me!
O Pritha's Son! whoso will turn to Me,
Though they be born from the very womb of Sin,
Woman or man; sprung of the Vaisya caste
Or lowly disregarded Sudra,--all
Plant foot upon the highest path; how then
The holy Brahmans and My Royal Saints?
Ah! ye who into this ill world are come--
Fleeting and false--set your faith fast on Me!
Fix heart and thought on Me! Adore Me! Bring
Offerings to Me! Make Me prostrations! Make
Me your supremest joy! and, undivided,
Unto My rest your spirits shall be guided.

HERE ENDS CHAPTER IX. OF THE BHAGAVAD-GITA,
Entitled "Rajavidyarajaguhyayog,"
Or "The Book of Religion by the Kingly Knowledge and the
Kingly
Mystery."

CHAPTER X

Krishna.[FN#16]
Hear farther yet, thou Long-Armed Lord! these latest words I say--
Uttered to bring thee bliss and peace, who lovest Me alway--
Not the great company of gods nor kingly Rishis know
My Nature, Who have made the gods and Rishis long ago;
He only knoweth-only he is free of sin, and wise,
Who seeth Me, Lord of the Worlds, with faith-enlightened eyes,
Unborn, undying, unbegun. Whatever Natures be
To mortal men distributed, those natures spring from Me!
Intellect, skill, enlightenment, endurance, self-control,
Truthfulness, equability, and grief or joy of soul,
And birth and death, and fearfulness, and fearlessness, and shame,
And honour, and sweet harmlessness,[FN#17] and peace which is the
same
Whate'er befalls, and mirth, and tears, and piety, and thrift,
And wish to give, and will to help,--all cometh of My gift!

The Seven Chief Saints, the Elders Four, the Lordly Manus set--
Sharing My work--to rule the worlds, these too did I beget;
And Rishis, Pitris, Manus, all, by one thought of My mind;
Thence did arise, to fill this world, the races of mankind;
Wherefrom who comprehends My Reign of mystic Majesty--
That truth of truths--is thenceforth linked in faultless faith to Me:
Yea! knowing Me the source of all, by Me all creatures wrought,
The wise in spirit cleave to Me, into My Being brought;
Hearts fixed on Me; breaths breathed to Me; praising Me, each to each,
So have they happiness and peace, with pious thought and speech;
And unto these--thus serving well, thus loving ceaselessly--
I give a mind of perfect mood, whereby they draw to Me;
And, all for love of them, within their darkened souls I dwell,
And, with bright rays of wisdom's lamp, their ignorance dispel.

Arjuna.

Yes! Thou art Parabrahm! The High Abode!
The Great Purification! Thou art God
Eternal, All-creating, Holy, First,
Without beginning! Lord of Lords and Gods!
Declared by all the Saints--by Narada,
Vyasa Asita, and Devalas;
And here Thyself declaring unto me!
What Thou hast said now know I to be truth,
O Kesava! that neither gods nor men
Nor demons comprehend Thy mystery
Made manifest, Divinest! Thou Thyself

Thyself alone dost know, Maker Supreme!
Master of all the living! Lord of Gods!
King of the Universe! To Thee alone
Belongs to tell the heavenly excellence
Of those perfections wherewith Thou dost fill
These worlds of Thine; Pervading, Immanent!
How shall I learn, Supremest Mystery!
To know Thee, though I muse continually?
Under what form of Thine unnumbered forms
Mayst Thou be grasped? Ah! yet again recount,
Clear and complete, Thy great appearances,
The secrets of Thy Majesty and Might,
Thou High Delight of Men! Never enough
Can mine ears drink the Amrit[FN#18] of such words!

Krishna.

Hanta! So be it! Kuru Prince! I will to thee unfold
Some portions of My Majesty, whose powers are manifold!
I am the Spirit seated deep in every creature's heart;
From Me they come; by Me they live; at My word they depart!
Vishnu of the Adityas I am, those Lords of Light;
Maritchi of the Maruts, the Kings of Storm and Blight;
By day I gleam, the golden Sun of burning cloudless Noon;
By Night, amid the asterisms I glide, the dappled Moon!
Of Vedas I am Sama-Ved, of gods in Indra's Heaven
Vasava; of the faculties to living beings given
The mind which apprehends and thinks; of Rudras Sankara;
Of Yakshas and of Rakshasas, Vittesh; and Pavaka
Of Vasus, and of mountain-peaks Meru; Vrihaspati
Know Me 'mid planetary Powers; 'mid Warriors heavenly
Skanda; of all the water-floods the Sea which drinketh each,
And Bhrigu of the holy Saints, and OM of sacred speech;
Of prayers the prayer ye whisper;[FN#19] of hills Himala's

snow,
And Aswattha, the fig-tree, of all the trees that grow;
Of the Devarshis, Narada; and Chitrarath of them
That sing in Heaven, and Kapila of Munis, and the gem
Of flying steeds, Uchchaisravas, from Amrit-wave which burst;
Of elephants Airavata; of males the Best and First;
Of weapons Heav'n's hot thunderbolt; of cows white Kama-dhuk,
From whose great milky udder-teats all hearts' desires are strook;
Vasuki of the serpent-tribes, round Mandara entwined;
And thousand-fanged Ananta, on whose broad coils reclined
Leans Vishnu; and of water-things Varuna; Aryam
Of Pitris, and, of those that judge, Yama the Judge I am;
Of Daityas dread Prahlada; of what metes days and years,
Time's self I am; of woodland-beasts-buffaloes, deers, and bears-
The lordly-painted tiger; of birds the vast Garud,
The whirlwind 'mid the winds; 'mid chiefs Rama with blood imbrued,
Makar 'mid fishes of the sea, and Ganges 'mid the streams;
Yea! First, and Last, and Centre of all which is or seems
I am, Arjuna! Wisdom Supreme of what is wise,
Words on the uttering lips I am, and eyesight of the eyes,
And "A" of written characters, Dwandwa[FN#20] of knitted speech,
And Endless Life, and boundless Love, whose power sustain-eth each;
And bitter Death which seizes all, and joyous sudden Birth,
Which brings to light all beings that are to be on earth;
And of the viewless virtues, Fame, Fortune, Song am I,
And Memory, and Patience; and Craft, and Constancy:

Of Vedic hymns the Vrihatsam, of metres Gayatri,
Of months the Margasirsha, of all the seasons three
The flower-wreathed Spring; in dicer's-play the conquering Double-Eight;
The splendour of the splendid, and the greatness of the great,
Victory I am, and Action! and the goodness of the good,
And Vasudev of Vrishni's race, and of this Pandu brood
Thyself!--Yea, my Arjuna! thyself; for thou art Mine!
Of poets Usana, of saints Vyasa, sage divine;
The policy of conquerors, the potency of kings,
The great unbroken silence in learning's secret things;
The lore of all the learned, the seed of all which springs.
Living or lifeless, still or stirred, whatever beings be,
None of them is in all the worlds, but it exists by Me!
Nor tongue can tell, Arjuna! nor end of telling come
Of these My boundless glories, whereof I teach thee some;
For wheresoe'er is wondrous work, and majesty, and might,
From Me hath all proceeded. Receive thou this aright!
Yet how shouldst thou receive, O Prince! the vastness of this word?
I, who am all, and made it all, abide its separate Lord!

HERE ENDETH CHAPTER X. OF THE BHAGAVAD-GITA,
Entitled "Vibhuti Yog,"
Or "The Book of Religion by the Heavenly Perfections."

CHAPTER XI

Arjuna.
This, for my soul's peace, have I heard from Thee,
The unfolding of the Mystery Supreme
Named Adhyatman; comprehending which,
My darkness is dispelled; for now I know--
O Lotus-eyed![FN#21]--whence is the birth of men,
And whence their death, and what the majesties
Of Thine immortal rule. Fain would I see,
As thou Thyself declar'st it, Sovereign Lord!
The likeness of that glory of Thy Form
Wholly revealed. O Thou Divinest One!
If this can be, if I may bear the sight,
Make Thyself visible, Lord of all prayers!
Show me Thy very self, the Eternal God!

Krishna.
Gaze, then, thou Son of Pritha! I manifest for thee
Those hundred thousand thousand shapes that clothe my Mystery:
I show thee all my semblances, infinite, rich, divine,
My changeful hues, my countless forms. See! in this face of mine,
Adityas, Vasus, Rudras, Aswins, and Maruts; see
Wonders unnumbered, Indian Prince! revealed to none save thee.
Behold! this is the Universe!--Look! what is live and dead
I gather all in one--in Me! Gaze, as thy lips have said,

On GOD ETERNAL, VERY GOD! See Me! see what thou prayest!

Thou canst not!--nor, with human eyes, Arjuna! ever mayest!
Therefore I give thee sense divine. Have other eyes, new light!
And, look! This is My glory, unveiled to mortal sight!

Sanjaya.
Then, O King! the God, so saying,
Stood, to Pritha's Son displaying
All the splendour, wonder, dread
Of His vast Almighty-head.
Out of countless eyes beholding,
Out of countless mouths commanding,
Countless mystic forms enfolding
In one Form: supremely standing
Countless radiant glories wearing,
Countless heavenly weapons bearing,
Crowned with garlands of star-clusters,
Robed in garb of woven lustres,
Breathing from His perfect Presence
Breaths of every subtle essence
Of all heavenly odours; shedding
Blinding brilliance; overspreading--
Boundless, beautiful--all spaces
With His all-regarding faces;
So He showed! If there should rise
Suddenly within the skies
Sunburst of a thousand suns
Flooding earth with beams undeemed-of,
Then might be that Holy One's
Majesty and radiance dreamed of!

So did Pandu's Son behold
All this universe enfold
All its huge diversity
Into one vast shape, and be
Visible, and viewed, and blended

In one Body--subtle, splendid,
Nameless--th' All-comprehending
God of Gods, the Never-Ending
Deity!

But, sore amazed,
Thrilled, o'erfilled, dazzled, and dazed,
Arjuna knelt; and bowed his head,
And clasped his palms; and cried, and said:

Arjuna.
Yea! I have seen! I see!
Lord! all is wrapped in Thee!
The gods are in Thy glorious frame! the creatures
Of earth, and heaven, and hell
In Thy Divine form dwell,
And in Thy countenance shine all the features

Of Brahma, sitting lone
Upon His lotus-throne;
Of saints and sages, and the serpent races
Ananta, Vasuki;
Yea! mightiest Lord! I see
Thy thousand thousand arms, and breasts, and faces,
And eyes,--on every side
Perfect, diversified;
And nowhere end of Thee, nowhere beginning,
Nowhere a centre! Shifts--
Wherever soul's gaze lifts--
Thy central Self, all-wielding, and all-winning!

Infinite King! I see
The anadem on Thee,
The club, the shell, the discus; see Thee burning
In beams insufferable,
Lighting earth, heaven, and hell
With brilliance blazing, glowing, flashing; turning

Darkness to dazzling day,
Look I whichever way;

Ah, Lord! I worship Thee, the Undivided,
The Uttermost of thought,
The Treasure-Palace wrought
To hold the wealth of the worlds; the Shield provided

To shelter Virtue's laws;
The Fount whence Life's stream draws
All waters of all rivers of all being:
The One Unborn, Unending:
Unchanging and Unblending!
With might and majesty, past thought, past seeing!

Silver of moon and gold
Of sun are glories rolled
From Thy great eyes; Thy visage, beaming tender
Throughout the stars and skies,
Doth to warm life surprise
Thy Universe. The worlds are filled with wonder

Of Thy perfections! Space
Star-sprinkled, and void place
From pole to pole of the Blue, from bound to bound,
Hath Thee in every spot,
Thee, Thee!--Where Thou art not,
O Holy, Marvellous Form! is nowhere found!

O Mystic, Awful One!
At sight of Thee, made known,
The Three Worlds quake; the lower gods draw nigh
Thee;
They fold their palms, and bow
Body, and breast, and brow,
And, whispering worship, laud and magnify Thee!

Rishis and Siddhas cry
"Hail! Highest Majesty!"
From sage and singer breaks the hymn of glory
In dulcet harmony,
Sounding the praise of Thee;
While countless companies take up the story,

Rudras, who ride the storms,
Th' Adityas' shining forms,
Vasus and Sadhyas, Viswas, Ushmapas;
Maruts, and those great Twins
The heavenly, fair, Aswins,
Gandharvas, Rakshasas, Siddhas, and Asuras,[FN#22]--

These see Thee, and revere
In sudden-stricken fear;
Yea! the Worlds,--seeing Thee with form stupendous,
With faces manifold,
With eyes which all behold,
Unnumbered eyes, vast arms, members tremendous,

Flanks, lit with sun and star,
Feet planted near and far,
Tushes of terror, mouths wrathful and tender;--
The Three wide Worlds before Thee
Adore, as I adore Thee,
Quake, as I quake, to witness so much splendour!

I mark Thee strike the skies
With front, in wondrous wise
Huge, rainbow-painted, glittering; and thy mouth
Opened, and orbs which see
All things, whatever be
In all Thy worlds, east, west, and north and south.

O Eyes of God! O Head!
My strength of soul is fled,
Gone is heart's force, rebuked is mind's desire!
When I behold Thee so,
With awful brows a-glow,
With burning glance, and lips lighted by fire

Fierce as those flames which shall
Consume, at close of all,
Earth, Heaven! Ah me! I see no Earth and Heaven!
Thee, Lord of Lords! I see,

Thee only-only Thee!
Now let Thy mercy unto me be given,

Thou Refuge of the World!
Lo! to the cavern hurled
Of Thy wide-opened throat, and lips white-tushed,
I see our noblest ones,
Great Dhritarashtra's sons,
Bhishma, Drona, and Karna, caught and crushed!

The Kings and Chiefs drawn in,
That gaping gorge within;
The best of both these armies torn and riven!
Between Thy jaws they lie
Mangled full bloodily,
Ground into dust and death! Like streams down-driven

With helpless haste, which go
In headlong furious flow
Straight to the gulfing deeps of th' unfilled ocean,
So to that flaming cave
Those heroes great and brave
Pour, in unending streams, with helpless motion!

Like moths which in the night
Flutter towards a light,
Drawn to their fiery doom, flying and dying,
So to their death still throng,
Blind, dazzled, borne along
Ceaselessly, all those multitudes, wild flying!

Thou, that hast fashioned men,
Devourest them again,
One with another, great and small, alike!
The creatures whom Thou mak'st,
With flaming jaws Thou tak'st,
Lapping them up! Lord God! Thy terrors strike

From end to end of earth,
Filling life full, from birth

To death, with deadly, burning, lurid dread!
Ah, Vishnu! make me know
Why is Thy visage so?
Who art Thou, feasting thus upon Thy dead?

Who? awful Deity!
I bow myself to Thee,
Namostu Te, Devavara! Prasid![FN#23]
O Mightiest Lord! rehearse
Why hast Thou face so fierce?
Whence doth this aspect horrible proceed?

Krishna.
Thou seest Me as Time who kills,
Time who brings all to doom,
The Slayer Time, Ancient of Days, come hither to consume;
Excepting thee, of all these hosts of hostile chiefs arrayed,
There stands not one shall leave alive the battlefield! Dismayed
No longer be! Arise! obtain renown! destroy thy foes!
Fight for the kingdom waiting thee when thou hast vanquished those.
By Me they fall--not thee! the stroke of death is dealt them now,
Even as they show thus gallantly; My instrument art thou!
Strike, strong-armed Prince, at Drona! at Bhishma strike! deal death
On Karna, Jyadratha; stay all their warlike breath!
'Tis I who bid them perish! Thou wilt but slay the slain;
Fight! they must fall, and thou must live, victor upon this plain!

Sanjaya.
Hearing mighty Keshav's word,
Tremblingly that helmed Lord
Clasped his lifted palms, and--praying
Grace of Krishna--stood there, saying,

With bowed brow and accents broken,
These words, timorously spoken:

Arjuna.
Worthily, Lord of Might!
The whole world hath delight
In Thy surpassing power, obeying Thee;
The Rakshasas, in dread
At sight of Thee, are sped
To all four quarters; and the company

Of Siddhas sound Thy name.
How should they not proclaim
Thy Majesties, Divinest, Mightiest?
Thou Brahm, than Brahma greater!
Thou Infinite Creator!
Thou God of gods, Life's Dwelling-place and Rest!

Thou, of all souls the Soul!
The Comprehending Whole!
Of being formed, and formless being the Framer;
O Utmost One! O Lord!
Older than eld, Who stored
The worlds with wealth of life! O Treasure-Claimer,

Who wottest all, and art
Wisdom Thyself! O Part
In all, and All; for all from Thee have risen
Numberless now I see
The aspects are of Thee!
Vayu[FN#24] Thou art, and He who keeps the prison

Of Narak, Yama dark;
And Agni's shining spark;
Varuna's waves are Thy waves. Moon and starlight
Are Thine! Prajapati
Art Thou, and 'tis to Thee
They knelt in worshipping the old world's far light,

The first of mortal men.
Again, Thou God! again
A thousand thousand times be magnified!
Honour and worship be--
Glory and praise,--to Thee
Namo, Namaste, cried on every side;

Cried here, above, below,
Uttered when Thou dost go,
Uttered where Thou dost come! Namo! we call;
Namostu! God adored!
Namostu! Nameless Lord!
Hail to Thee! Praise to Thee! Thou One in all;

For Thou art All! Yea, Thou!
Ah! if in anger now
Thou shouldst remember I did think Thee Friend,
Speaking with easy speech,
As men use each to each;
Did call Thee "Krishna," "Prince," nor comprehend

Thy hidden majesty,
The might, the awe of Thee;
Did, in my heedlessness, or in my love,
On journey, or in jest,
Or when we lay at rest,
Sitting at council, straying in the grove,

Alone, or in the throng,
Do Thee, most Holy! wrong,
Be Thy grace granted for that witless sin!
For Thou art, now I know,
Father of all below,
Of all above, of all the worlds within

Guru of Gurus; more
To reverence and adore
Than all which is adorable and high!
How, in the wide worlds three

Should any equal be?
Should any other share Thy Majesty?

Therefore, with body bent
And reverent intent,
I praise, and serve, and seek Thee, asking grace.
As father to a son,
As friend to friend, as one
Who loveth to his lover, turn Thy face

In gentleness on me!
Good is it I did see
This unknown marvel of Thy Form! But fear
Mingles with joy! Retake,
Dear Lord! for pity's sake
Thine earthly shape, which earthly eyes may bear!

Be merciful, and show
The visage that I know;
Let me regard Thee, as of yore, arrayed
With disc and forehead-gem,
With mace and anadem,
Thou that sustainest all things! Undismayed

Let me once more behold
The form I loved of old,
Thou of the thousand arms and countless eyes!
This frightened heart is fain
To see restored again
My Charioteer, in Krishna's kind disguise.

Krishna.
Yea! thou hast seen, Arjuna! because I loved thee well,
The secret countenance of Me, revealed by mystic spell,
Shining, and wonderful, and vast, majestic, manifold,
Which none save thou in all the years had favour to behold;
For not by Vedas cometh this, nor sacrifice, nor alms,
Nor works well-done, nor penance long, nor prayers,

nor chaunted
psalms,
That mortal eyes should bear to view the Immortal Soul unclad,
Prince of the Kurus! This was kept for thee alone! Be glad!
Let no more trouble shake thy heart, because thine eyes have seen
My terror with My glory. As I before have been
So will I be again for thee; with lightened heart behold!
Once more I am thy Krishna, the form thou knew'st of old!

Sanjaya.
These words to Arjuna spake
Vasudev, and straight did take
Back again the semblance dear
Of the well-loved charioteer;
Peace and joy it did restore
When the Prince beheld once more
Mighty BRAHMA's form and face
Clothed in Krishna's gentle grace.

Arjuna.
Now that I see come back, Janardana!
This friendly human frame, my mind can think
Calm thoughts once more; my heart beats still again!

Krishna.
Yea! it was wonderful and terrible
To view me as thou didst, dear Prince! The gods
Dread and desire continually to view!
Yet not by Vedas, nor from sacrifice,
Nor penance, nor gift-giving, nor with prayer
Shall any so behold, as thou hast seen!
Only by fullest service, perfect faith,
And uttermost surrender am I known
And seen, and entered into, Indian Prince!
Who doeth all for Me; who findeth Me
In all; adoreth always; loveth all

Which I have made, and Me, for Love's sole end
That man, Arjuna! unto Me doth wend.

HERE ENDETH CHAPTER XI. OF THE BHAGAVAD-GITA,
Entitled "Viswarupadarsanam,"
Or "The Book of the Manifesting of the One and Manifold."

CHAPTER XII

Arjuna.

Lord! of the men who serve Thee--true in heart--
As God revealed; and of the men who serve,
Worshipping Thee Unrevealed, Unbodied, Far,
Which take the better way of faith and life?

Krishna.

Whoever serve Me--as I show Myself--
Constantly true, in full devotion fixed,
Those hold I very holy. But who serve--
Worshipping Me The One, The Invisible,
The Unrevealed, Unnamed, Unthinkable,
Uttermost, All-pervading, Highest, Sure--
Who thus adore Me, mastering their sense,
Of one set mind to all, glad in all good,
These blessed souls come unto Me.

Yet, hard
The travail is for such as bend their minds
To reach th' Unmanifest That viewless path
Shall scarce be trod by man bearing the flesh!
But whereso any doeth all his deeds

Renouncing self for Me, full of Me, fixed
To serve only the Highest, night and day
Musing on Me--him will I swiftly lift
Forth from life's ocean of distress and death,
Whose soul clings fast to Me. Cling thou to Me!
Clasp Me with heart and mind! so shalt thou dwell
Surely with Me on high. But if thy thought
Droops from such height; if thou be'st weak to set
Body and soul upon Me constantly,
Despair not! give Me lower service! seek
To reach Me, worshipping with steadfast will;
And, if thou canst not worship steadfastly,
Work for Me, toil in works pleasing to Me!
For he that laboureth right for love of Me
Shall finally attain! But, if in this
Thy faint heart fails, bring Me thy failure! find
Refuge in Me! let fruits of labour go,
Renouncing hope for Me, with lowliest heart,
So shalt thou come; for, though to know is more
Than diligence, yet worship better is
Than knowing, and renouncing better still.
Near to renunciation--very near--
Dwelleth Eternal Peace!

Who hateth nought
Of all which lives, living himself benign,
Compassionate, from arrogance exempt,
Exempt from love of self, unchangeable
By good or ill; patient, contented, firm
In faith, mastering himself, true to his word,
Seeking Me, heart and soul; vowed unto Me,--
That man I love! Who troubleth not his kind,
And is not troubled by them; clear of wrath,
Living too high for gladness, grief, or fear,

That man I love! Who, dwelling quiet-eyed,[FN#25]
Stainless, serene, well-balanced, unperplexed,
Working with Me, yet from all works detached,
That man I love! Who, fixed in faith on Me,
Dotes upon none, scorns none; rejoices not,
And grieves not, letting good or evil hap
Light when it will, and when it will depart,
That man I love! Who, unto friend and foe
Keeping an equal heart, with equal mind
Bears shame and glory; with an equal peace
Takes heat and cold, pleasure and pain; abides
Quit of desires, hears praise or calumny
In passionless restraint, unmoved by each;
Linked by no ties to earth, steadfast in Me,
That man I love! But most of all I love
Those happy ones to whom 'tis life to live
In single fervid faith and love unseeing,
Drinking the blessed Amrit of my Being!

HERE ENDETH CHAPTER XII. OF THE BHAGAVAD-GITA,
Entitled "Bhaktiyog,"
Or"The Book of the Religion of Faith."

CHAPTER XIII

Arjuna.
Now would I hear, O gracious Kesava![FN#26]
Of Life which seems, and Soul beyond, which sees,
And what it is we know-or think to know.
Krishna.
Yea! Son of Kunti! for this flesh ye see
Is Kshetra, is the field where Life disports;
And that which views and knows it is the Soul,
Kshetrajna. In all "fields," thou Indian prince!
I am Kshetrajna. I am what surveys!
Only that knowledge knows which knows the known
By the knower![FN#27] What it is, that "field" of life,
What qualities it hath, and whence it is,
And why it changeth, and the faculty
That wotteth it, the mightiness of this,
And how it wotteth-hear these things from Me!
............[FN#28]
The elements, the conscious life, the mind,
The unseen vital force, the nine strange gates
Of the body, and the five domains of sense;

Desire, dislike, pleasure and pain, and thought
Deep-woven, and persistency of being;
These all are wrought on Matter by the Soul!

Humbleness, truthfulness, and harmlessness,
Patience and honour, reverence for the wise.
Purity, constancy, control of self,
Contempt of sense-delights, self-sacrifice,
Perception of the certitude of ill
In birth, death, age, disease, suffering, and sin;
Detachment, lightly holding unto home,
Children, and wife, and all that bindeth men;
An ever-tranquil heart in fortunes good
And fortunes evil, with a will set firm
To worship Me--Me only! ceasing not;
Loving all solitudes, and shunning noise
Of foolish crowds; endeavours resolute
To reach perception of the Utmost Soul,
And grace to understand what gain it were
So to attain,--this is true Wisdom, Prince!
And what is otherwise is ignorance!

Now will I speak of knowledge best to know-
That Truth which giveth man Amrit to drink,
The Truth of HIM, the Para-Brahm, the All,
The Uncreated;; not Asat, not Sat,
Not Form, nor the Unformed; yet both, and more;--
Whose hands are everywhere, and everywhere
Planted His feet, and everywhere His eyes
Beholding, and His ears in every place
Hearing, and all His faces everywhere
Enlightening and encompassing His worlds.
Glorified in the senses He hath given,
Yet beyond sense He is; sustaining all,
Yet dwells He unattached: of forms and modes

Master, yet neither form nor mode hath He;
He is within all beings--and without--
Motionless, yet still moving; not discerned
For subtlety of instant presence; close
To all, to each; yet measurelessly far!
Not manifold, and yet subsisting still
In all which lives; for ever to be known
As the Sustainer, yet, at the End of Times,
He maketh all to end--and re-creates.
The Light of Lights He is, in the heart of the Dark
Shining eternally. Wisdom He is
And Wisdom's way, and Guide of all the wise,
Planted in every heart.

So have I told
Of Life's stuff, and the moulding, and the lore
To comprehend. Whoso, adoring Me,
Perceiveth this, shall surely come to Me!

Know thou that Nature and the Spirit both
Have no beginning! Know that qualities
And changes of them are by Nature wrought;
That Nature puts to work the acting frame,
But Spirit doth inform it, and so cause
Feeling of pain and pleasure. Spirit, linked
To moulded matter, entereth into bond
With qualities by Nature framed, and, thus
Married to matter, breeds the birth again
In good or evil yonis.[FN#29]

Yet is this
Yea! in its bodily prison!--Spirit pure,
Spirit supreme; surveying, governing,
Guarding, possessing; Lord and Master still
PURUSHA, Ultimate, One Soul with Me.

Whoso thus knows himself, and knows his soul
PURUSHA, working through the qualities
With Nature's modes, the light hath come for him!
Whatever flesh he bears, never again
Shall he take on its load. Some few there be
By meditation find the Soul in Self
Self-schooled; and some by long philosophy
And holy life reach thither; some by works:
Some, never so attaining, hear of light
From other lips, and seize, and cleave to it
Worshipping; yea! and those--to teaching true--
Overpass Death!

Wherever, Indian Prince!
Life is--of moving things, or things unmoved,
Plant or still seed--know, what is there hath grown
By bond of Matter and of Spirit: Know
He sees indeed who sees in all alike
The living, lordly Soul; the Soul Supreme,
Imperishable amid the Perishing:
For, whoso thus beholds, in every place,
In every form, the same, one, Living Life,
Doth no more wrongfulness unto himself,
But goes the highest road which brings to bliss.
Seeing, he sees, indeed, who sees that works
Are Nature's wont, for Soul to practise by
Acting, yet not the agent; sees the mass
Of separate living things--each of its kind--
Issue from One, and blend again to One:
Then hath he BRAHMA, he attains!

O Prince!
That Ultimate, High Spirit, Uncreate,
Unqualified, even when it entereth flesh
Taketh no stain of acts, worketh in nought!

Like to the ethereal air, pervading all,
Which, for sheer subtlety, avoideth taint,
The subtle Soul sits everywhere, unstained:
Like to the light of the all-piercing sun
[Which is not changed by aught it shines upon,]
The Soul's light shineth pure in every place;
And they who, by such eye of wisdom, see
How Matter, and what deals with it, divide;
And how the Spirit and the flesh have strife,
Those wise ones go the way which leads to Life!

HERE ENDS CHAPTER XIII. OF THE BHAGAVAD-GITA,
Entitled "Kshetrakshetrajnavibhagayog,"
Or "The Book of Religion by Separation of Matter and Spirit."

CHAPTER XIV

Krishna.

Yet farther will I open unto thee
This wisdom of all wisdoms, uttermost,
The which possessing, all My saints have passed
To perfectness. On such high verities
Reliant, rising into fellowship
With Me, they are not born again at birth
Of Kalpas, nor at Pralyas suffer change!

This Universe the womb is where I plant
Seed of all lives! Thence, Prince of India, comes
Birth to all beings! Whoso, Kunti's Son!
Mothers each mortal form, Brahma conceives,
And I am He that fathers, sending seed!

Sattwan, Rajas, and Tamas, so are named
The qualities of Nature, "Soothfastness,"
"Passion," and "Ignorance." These three bind down
The changeless Spirit in the changeful flesh.
Whereof sweet "Soothfastness," by purity
Living unsullied and enlightened, binds
The sinless Soul to happiness and truth;
And Passion, being kin to appetite,
And breeding impulse and propensity,

Binds the embodied Soul, O Kunti's Son!
By tie of works. But Ignorance, begot
Of Darkness, blinding mortal men, binds down
Their souls to stupor, sloth, and drowsiness.
Yea, Prince of India! Soothfastness binds souls
In pleasant wise to flesh; and Passion binds
By toilsome strain; but Ignorance, which blots
The beams of wisdom, binds the soul to sloth.
Passion and Ignorance, once overcome,
Leave Soothfastness, O Bharata! Where this
With Ignorance are absent, Passion rules;
And Ignorance in hearts not good nor quick.
When at all gateways of the Body shines
The Lamp of Knowledge, then may one see well
Soothfastness settled in that city reigns;
Where longing is, and ardour, and unrest,
Impulse to strive and gain, and avarice,
Those spring from Passion--Prince!--engrained; and where
Darkness and dulness, sloth and stupor are,
'Tis Ignorance hath caused them, Kuru Chief!

Moreover, when a soul departeth, fixed
In Soothfastness, it goeth to the place--
Perfect and pure--of those that know all Truth.
If it departeth in set habitude
Of Impulse, it shall pass into the world
Of spirits tied to works; and, if it dies
In hardened Ignorance, that blinded soul
Is born anew in some unlighted womb.

The fruit of Soothfastness is true and sweet;
The fruit of lusts is pain and toil; the fruit
Of Ignorance is deeper darkness. Yea!
For Light brings light, and Passion ache to have;
And gloom, bewilderments, and ignorance

Grow forth from Ignorance. Those of the first
Rise ever higher; those of the second mode
Take a mid place; the darkened souls sink back
To lower deeps, loaded with witlessness!

When, watching life, the living man perceives
The only actors are the Qualities,
And knows what rules beyond the Qualities,
Then is he come nigh unto Me!

The Soul,
Thus passing forth from the Three Qualities--
Whereby arise all bodies--overcomes
Birth, Death, Sorrow, and Age; and drinketh deep
The undying wine of Amrit.

Arjuna.
Oh, my Lord!
Which be the signs to know him that hath gone
Past the Three Modes? How liveth he? What way
Leadeth him safe beyond the threefold Modes?

Krishna.
He who with equanimity surveys
Lustre of goodness, strife of passion, sloth
Of ignorance, not angry if they are,
Not wishful when they are not: he who sits
A sojourner and stranger in their midst
Unruffled, standing off, saying--serene--
When troubles break, "These be the Qualities!"
He unto whom--self-centred--grief and joy
Sound as one word; to whose deep-seeing eyes
The clod, the marble, and the gold are one;
Whose equal heart holds the same gentleness
For lovely and unlovely things, firm-set,
Well-pleased in praise and dispraise; satisfied
With honour or dishonour; unto friends

And unto foes alike in tolerance;
Detached from undertakings,--he is named
Surmounter of the Qualities!
    And such--
With single, fervent faith adoring Me,
Passing beyond the Qualities, conforms
To Brahma, and attains Me!
    For I am
That whereof Brahma is the likeness! Mine
The Amrit is; and Immortality
Is mine; and mine perfect Felicity!

HERE ENDS CHAPTER XIV. OF THE BHAGAVAD-GITA

Entitled "Gunatrayavibhagayog,"

Or "The Book of Religion by Separation from the Qualities."

CHAPTER XV

Krishna.
Men call the Aswattha,--the Banyan-tree,--
Which hath its boughs beneath, its roots above,--
The ever-holy tree. Yea! for its leaves
Are green and waving hymns which whisper Truth!
Who knows the Aswattha, knows Veds, and all.
Its branches shoot to heaven and sink to earth,[FN#30]
Even as the deeds of men, which take their birth
From qualities: its silver sprays and blooms,
And all the eager verdure of its girth,
Leap to quick life at kiss of sun and air,
As men's lives quicken to the temptings fair
Of wooing sense: its hanging rootlets seek
The soil beneath, helping to hold it there,
As actions wrought amid this world of men
Bind them by ever-tightening bonds again.
If ye knew well the teaching of the Tree,
What its shape saith; and whence it springs; and, then
How it must end, and all the ills of it,
The axe of sharp Detachment ye would whet,

And cleave the clinging snaky roots, and lay
This Aswattha of sense-life low,--to set
New growths upspringing to that happier sky,--
Which they who reach shall have no day to die,
Nor fade away, nor fall--to Him, I mean,
FATHER and FIRST, Who made the mystery
Of old Creation; for to Him come they
From passion and from dreams who break away;
Who part the bonds constraining them to flesh,
And,--Him, the Highest, worshipping alway--
No longer grow at mercy of what breeze
Of summer pleasure stirs the sleeping trees,
What blast of tempest tears them, bough and stem
To the eternal world pass such as these!
Another Sun gleams there! another Moon!
Another Light,--not Dusk, nor Dawn, nor Noon--
Which they who once behold return no more;
They have attained My rest, life's Utmost boon!
When, in this world of manifested life,
The undying Spirit, setting forth from Me,
Taketh on form, it draweth to itself
From Being's storehouse,--which containeth all,--
Senses and intellect. The Sovereign Soul
Thus entering the flesh, or quitting it,
Gathers these up, as the wind gathers scents,
Blowing above the flower-beds. Ear and Eye,
And Touch and Taste, and Smelling, these it takes,--
Yea, and a sentient mind;--linking itself
To sense-things so.
The unenlightened ones
Mark not that Spirit when he goes or comes,
Nor when he takes his pleasure in the form,
Conjoined with qualities; but those see plain

Who have the eyes to see. Holy souls see
Which strive thereto. Enlightened, they perceive
That Spirit in themselves; but foolish ones,
Even though they strive, discern not, having hearts
Unkindled, ill-informed!
    Know, too, from Me
Shineth the gathered glory of the suns
Which lighten all the world: from Me the moons
Draw silvery beams, and fire fierce loveliness.
I penetrate the clay, and lend all shapes
Their living force; I glide into the plant--
Root, leaf, and bloom--to make the woodlands green
With springing sap. Becoming vital warmth,
I glow in glad, respiring frames, and pass,
With outward and with inward breath, to feed
The body by all meats.[FN#31]
    For in this world
Being is twofold: the Divided, one;
The Undivided, one. All things that live
Are "the Divided." That which sits apart,
"The Undivided."
    Higher still is He,
The Highest, holding all, whose Name is LORD,
The Eternal, Sovereign, First! Who fills all worlds,
Sustaining them. And--dwelling thus beyond
Divided Being and Undivided--I
Am called of men and Vedas, Life Supreme,
The PURUSHOTTAMA.
    Who knows Me thus,
With mind unclouded, knoweth all, dear Prince!
And with his whole soul ever worshippeth Me.

Now is the sacred, secret Mystery
Declared to thee! Who comprehendeth this
Hath wisdom! He is quit of works in bliss!

HERE ENDS CHAPTER XV. OF THE BHAGAVAD-GITA
Entitled "Purushottamapraptiyog,"
Or "The Book of Religion by attaining the Supreme."

CHAPTER XVI

Krishna.

Fearlessness, singleness of soul, the will
Always to strive for wisdom; opened hand
And governed appetites; and piety,
And love of lonely study; humbleness,
Uprightness, heed to injure nought which lives,
Truthfulness, slowness unto wrath, a mind
That lightly letteth go what others prize;
And equanimity, and charity
Which spieth no man's faults; and tenderness
Towards all that suffer; a contented heart,
Fluttered by no desires; a bearing mild,
Modest, and grave, with manhood nobly mixed,
With patience, fortitude, and purity;
An unrevengeful spirit, never given
To rate itself too high;--such be the signs,
O Indian Prince! of him whose feet are set
On that fair path which leads to heavenly birth!

Deceitfulness, and arrogance, and pride,
Quickness to anger, harsh and evil speech,
And ignorance, to its own darkness blind,--
These be the signs, My Prince! of him whose birth
Is fated for the regions of the vile.[FN#32]

The Heavenly Birth brings to deliverance,
So should'st thou know! The birth with Asuras
Brings into bondage. Be thou joyous, Prince!
Whose lot is set apart for heavenly Birth.

Two stamps there are marked on all living men,
Divine and Undivine; I spake to thee
By what marks thou shouldst know the Heavenly Man,
Hear from me now of the Unheavenly!

They comprehend not, the Unheavenly,
How Souls go forth from Me; nor how they come
Back unto Me: nor is there Truth in these,
Nor purity, nor rule of Life. "This world
Hath not a Law, nor Order, nor a Lord,"
So say they: "nor hath risen up by Cause
Following on Cause, in perfect purposing,
But is none other than a House of Lust."
And, this thing thinking, all those ruined ones--
Of little wit, dark-minded--give themselves
To evil deeds, the curses of their kind.
Surrendered to desires insatiable,
Full of deceitfulness, folly, and pride,
In blindness cleaving to their errors, caught
Into the sinful course, they trust this lie
As it were true--this lie which leads to death--
Finding in Pleasure all the good which is,
And crying "Here it finisheth!"

Ensnared
In nooses of a hundred idle hopes,
Slaves to their passion and their wrath, they buy
Wealth with base deeds, to glut hot appetites;
"Thus much, to-day," they say, "we gained! thereby
Such and such wish of heart shall have its fill;
And this is ours! and th' other shall be ours!

To-day we slew a foe, and we will slay
Our other enemy to-morrow! Look!
Are we not lords? Make we not goodly cheer?
Is not our fortune famous, brave, and great?
Rich are we, proudly born! What other men
Live like to us? Kill, then, for sacrifice!
Cast largesse, and be merry!" So they speak
Darkened by ignorance; and so they fall--
Tossed to and fro with projects, tricked, and bound
In net of black delusion, lost in lusts--
Down to foul Naraka. Conceited, fond,
Stubborn and proud, dead-drunken with the wine
Of wealth, and reckless, all their offerings
Have but a show of reverence, being not made
In piety of ancient faith. Thus vowed
To self-hood, force, insolence, feasting, wrath,
These My blasphemers, in the forms they wear
And in the forms they breed, my foemen are,
Hateful and hating; cruel, evil, vile,
Lowest and least of men, whom I cast down
Again, and yet again, at end of lives,
Into some devilish womb, whence--birth by birth--
The devilish wombs re-spawn them, all beguiled;
And, till they find and worship Me, sweet Prince!
Tread they that Nether Road.
    The Doors of Hell
Are threefold, whereby men to ruin pass,--
The door of Lust, the door of Wrath, the door
Of Avarice. Let a man shun those three!
He who shall turn aside from entering
All those three gates of Narak, wendeth straight
To find his peace, and comes to Swarga's gate.
    . . . .[FN#33]

HERE ENDETH CHAPTER XVI. OF THE BHAGAVAD-GITA,
Entitled "Daivasarasaupadwibhagayog,"
Or "The Book of the Separateness of the Divine and Undivine."

CHAPTER XVII

Arjuna.
If men forsake the holy ordinance,
Heedless of Shastras, yet keep faith at heart
And worship, what shall be the state of those,
Great Krishna! Sattwan, Rajas, Tamas? Say!
Krishna.
Threefold the faith is of mankind and springs
From those three qualities,--becoming "true,"
Or "passion-stained," or "dark," as thou shalt hear!
The faith of each believer, Indian Prince!
Conforms itself to what he truly is.
Where thou shalt see a worshipper, that one
To what he worships lives assimilate,
[Such as the shrine, so is the votary,]
The "soothfast" souls adore true gods; the souls
Obeying Rajas worship Rakshasas[FN#34]
Or Yakshas; and the men of Darkness pray
To Pretas and to Bhutas.[FN#35] Yea, and those
Who practise bitter penance, not enjoined
By rightful rule--penance which hath its root
In self-sufficient, proud hypocrisies--
Those men, passion-beset, violent, wild,
Torturing--the witless ones--My elements
Shut in fair company within their flesh,

(Nay, Me myself, present within the flesh!)
Know them to devils devoted, not to Heaven!
For like as foods are threefold for mankind
In nourishing, so is there threefold way
Of worship, abstinence, and almsgiving!
Hear this of Me! there is a food which brings
Force, substance, strength, and health, and joy to live,
Being well-seasoned, cordial, comforting,
The "Soothfast" meat. And there be foods which bring
Aches and unrests, and burning blood, and grief,
Being too biting, heating, salt, and sharp,
And therefore craved by too strong appetite.
And there is foul food--kept from over-night,[FN#36]
Savourless, filthy, which the foul will eat,
A feast of rottenness, meet for the lips
Of such as love the "Darkness."

Thus with rites;--
A sacrifice not for rewardment made,
Offered in rightful wise, when he who vows
Sayeth, with heart devout, "This I should do!"
Is "Soothfast" rite. But sacrifice for gain,
Offered for good repute, be sure that this,
O Best of Bharatas! is Rajas-rite,
With stamp of "passion." And a sacrifice
Offered against the laws, with no due dole
Of food-giving, with no accompaniment
Of hallowed hymn, nor largesse to the priests,
In faithless celebration, call it vile,
The deed of "Darkness!"--lost!

Worship of gods
Meriting worship; lowly reverence
Of Twice-borns, Teachers, Elders; Purity,
Rectitude, and the Brahmacharya's vow,

And not to injure any helpless thing,--
These make a true religiousness of Act.
    Words causing no man woe, words ever true,
Gentle and pleasing words, and those ye say
In murmured reading of a Sacred Writ,--
These make the true religiousness of Speech.
    Serenity of soul, benignity,
Sway of the silent Spirit, constant stress
To sanctify the Nature,--these things make
Good rite, and true religiousness of Mind.
    Such threefold faith, in highest piety
Kept, with no hope of gain, by hearts devote,
Is perfect work of Sattwan, true belief.
    Religion shown in act of proud display
To win good entertainment, worship, fame,
Such--say I--is of Rajas, rash and vain.
    Religion followed by a witless will
To torture self, or come at power to hurt
Another,--'tis of Tamas, dark and ill.
    The gift lovingly given, when one shall say
"Now must I gladly give!" when he who takes
Can render nothing back; made in due place,
Due time, and to a meet recipient,
Is gift of Sattwan, fair and profitable.
    The gift selfishly given, where to receive
Is hoped again, or when some end is sought,
Or where the gift is proffered with a grudge,
This is of Rajas, stained with impulse, ill.
    The gift churlishly flung, at evil time,
In wrongful place, to base recipient,
Made in disdain or harsh unkindliness,
Is gift of Tamas, dark; it doth not bless![FN#37]

HERE ENDETH CHAPTER XVII. OF THE BHAGAVAD-GITA,
Entitled "Sraddhatrayavibhagayog,"
Or "The Book of Religion by the Threefold Kinds of Faith."

CHAPTER XVIII

Arjuna.
Fain would I better know, Thou Glorious One!
The very truth--Heart's Lord!--of Sannyas,
Abstention; and enunciation, Lord!
Tyaga; and what separates these twain!
Krishna.
The poets rightly teach that Sannyas
Is the foregoing of all acts which spring
Out of desire; and their wisest say
Tyaga is renouncing fruit of acts.
There be among the saints some who have held
All action sinful, and to be renounced;
And some who answer, "Nay! the goodly acts--
As worship, penance, alms--must be performed!"
Hear now My sentence, Best of Bharatas!
'Tis well set forth, O Chaser of thy Foes!
Renunciation is of threefold form,
And Worship, Penance, Alms, not to be stayed;
Nay, to be gladly done; for all those three
Are purifying waters for true souls!
Yet must be practised even those high works
In yielding up attachment, and all fruit
Produced by works. This is My judgment, Prince!
This My insuperable and fixed decree!

Abstaining from a work by right prescribed
Never is meet! So to abstain doth spring
From "Darkness," and Delusion teacheth it.
Abstaining from a work grievous to flesh,
When one saith "'Tis unpleasing!" this is null!
Such an one acts from "passion;" nought of gain
Wins his Renunciation! But, Arjun!
Abstaining from attachment to the work,
Abstaining from rewardment in the work,
While yet one doeth it full faithfully,
Saying, "Tis right to do!" that is "true " act
And abstinence! Who doeth duties so,
Unvexed if his work fail, if it succeed
Unflattered, in his own heart justified,
Quit of debates and doubts, his is "true" act:
For, being in the body, none may stand
Wholly aloof from act; yet, who abstains
From profit of his acts is abstinent.

The fruit of labours, in the lives to come,
Is threefold for all men,--Desirable,
And Undesirable, and mixed of both;
But no fruit is at all where no work was.

Hear from me, Long-armed Lord! the makings five
Which go to every act, in Sankhya taught
As necessary. First the force; and then
The agent; next, the various instruments;
Fourth, the especial effort; fifth, the God.
What work soever any mortal doth
Of body, mind, or speech, evil or good,
By these five doth he that. Which being thus,
Whoso, for lack of knowledge, seeth himself
As the sole actor, knoweth nought at all
And seeth nought. Therefore, I say, if one--

Holding aloof from self--with unstained mind
Should slay all yonder host, being bid to slay,
He doth not slay; he is not bound thereby!

Knowledge, the thing known, and the mind which knows,
These make the threefold starting-ground of act.
The act, the actor, and the instrument,
These make the threefold total of the deed.
But knowledge, agent, act, are differenced
By three dividing qualities. Hear now
Which be the qualities dividing them.

There is "true" Knowledge. Learn thou it is this:
To see one changeless Life in all the Lives,
And in the Separate, One Inseparable.
There is imperfect Knowledge: that which sees
The separate existences apart,
And, being separated, holds them real.
There is false Knowledge: that which blindly clings
To one as if 'twere all, seeking no Cause,
Deprived of light, narrow, and dull, and "dark."

There is "right" Action: that which being enjoined--
Is wrought without attachment, passionlessly,
For duty, not for love, nor hate, nor gain.
There is "vain" Action: that which men pursue
Aching to satisfy desires, impelled
By sense of self, with all-absorbing stress:
This is of Rajas--passionate and vain.
There is "dark" Action: when one doth a thing
Heedless of issues, heedless of the hurt
Or wrong for others, heedless if he harm
His own soul--'tis of Tamas, black and bad!

There is the "rightful"doer. He who acts
Free from self-seeking, humble, resolute,
Steadfast, in good or evil hap the same,

Content to do aright-he "truly" acts.
There is th' "impassioned" doer. He that works
From impulse, seeking profit, rude and bold
To overcome, unchastened; slave by turns
Of sorrow and of joy: of Rajas he!
And there be evil doers; loose of heart,
Low-minded, stubborn, fraudulent, remiss,
Dull, slow, despondent--children of the "dark."

Hear, too, of Intellect and Steadfastness
The threefold separation, Conqueror-Prince!
How these are set apart by Qualities.

Good is the Intellect which comprehends
The coming forth and going back of life,
What must be done, and what must not be done,
What should be feared, and what should not be feared,
What binds and what emancipates the soul:
That is of Sattwan, Prince! of "soothfastness."
Marred is the Intellect which, knowing right
And knowing wrong, and what is well to do
And what must not be done, yet understands
Nought with firm mind, nor as the calm truth is:
This is of Rajas, Prince! and "passionate!"
Evil is Intellect which, wrapped in gloom,
Looks upon wrong as right, and sees all things
Contrariwise of Truth. O Pritha's Son!
That is of Tamas, "dark" and desperate!

Good is the steadfastness whereby a man
Masters his beats of heart, his very breath
Of life, the action of his senses; fixed
In never-shaken faith and piety:
That is of Sattwan, Prince! "soothfast" and fair!
Stained is the steadfastness whereby a man
Holds to his duty, purpose, effort, end,

For life's sake, and the love of goods to gain,
Arjuna! 'tis of Rajas, passion-stamped!
Sad is the steadfastness wherewith the fool
Cleaves to his sloth, his sorrow, and his fears,
His folly and despair. This--Pritha's Son!--
Is born of Tamas, "dark" and miserable!

Hear further, Chief of Bharatas! from Me
The threefold kinds of Pleasure which there be.

Good Pleasure is the pleasure that endures,
Banishing pain for aye; bitter at first
As poison to the soul, but afterward
Sweet as the taste of Amrit. Drink of that!
It springeth in the Spirit's deep content.
And painful Pleasure springeth from the bond
Between the senses and the sense-world. Sweet
As Amrit is its first taste, but its last
Bitter as poison. 'Tis of Rajas, Prince!
And foul and "dark" the Pleasure is which springs
From sloth and sin and foolishness; at first
And at the last, and all the way of life
The soul bewildering. 'Tis of Tamas, Prince!

For nothing lives on earth, nor 'midst the gods
In utmost heaven, but hath its being bound
With these three Qualities, by Nature framed.

The work of Brahmans, Kshatriyas, Vaisyas,
And Sudras, O thou Slayer of thy Foes!
Is fixed by reason of the Qualities
Planted in each:

A Brahman's virtues, Prince!
Born of his nature, are serenity,
Self-mastery, religion, purity,
Patience, uprightness, learning, and to know
The truth of things which be. A Kshatriya's pride,

Born of his nature, lives in valour, fire,
Constancy, skilfulness, spirit in fight,
And open-handedness and noble mien,
As of a lord of men. A Vaisya's task,
Born with his nature, is to till the ground,
Tend cattle, venture trade. A Sudra's state,
Suiting his nature, is to minister.

Whoso performeth--diligent, content--
The work allotted him, whate'er it be,
Lays hold of perfectness! Hear how a man
Findeth perfection, being so content:
He findeth it through worship--wrought by work--
Of Him that is the Source of all which lives,
Of HIM by Whom the universe was stretched.

Better thine own work is, though done with fault,
Than doing others' work, ev'n excellently.
He shall not fall in sin who fronts the task
Set him by Nature's hand! Let no man leave
His natural duty, Prince! though it bear blame!
For every work hath blame, as every flame
Is wrapped in smoke! Only that man attains
Perfect surcease of work whose work was wrought
With mind unfettered, soul wholly subdued,
Desires for ever dead, results renounced.

Learn from me, Son of Kunti! also this,
How one, attaining perfect peace, attains
BRAHM, the supreme, the highest height of all!

Devoted--with a heart grown pure, restrained
In lordly self-control, forgoing wiles
Of song and senses, freed from love and hate,
Dwelling 'mid solitudes, in diet spare,
With body, speech, and will tamed to obey,
Ever to holy meditation vowed,

From passions liberate, quit of the Self,
Of arrogance, impatience, anger, pride;
Freed from surroundings, quiet, lacking nought--
Such an one grows to oneness with the BRAHM;
Such an one, growing one with BRAHM, serene,
Sorrows no more, desires no more; his soul,
Equally loving all that lives, loves well
Me, Who have made them, and attains to Me.
By this same love and worship doth he know
Me as I am, how high and wonderful,
And knowing, straightway enters into Me.
And whatsoever deeds he doeth--fixed
In Me, as in his refuge--he hath won
For ever and for ever by My grace
Th' Eternal Rest! So win thou! In thy thoughts
Do all thou dost for Me! Renounce for Me!
Sacrifice heart and mind and will to Me!
Live in the faith of Me! In faith of Me
All dangers thou shalt vanquish, by My grace;
But, trusting to thyself and heeding not,
Thou can'st but perish! If this day thou say'st,
Relying on thyself, "I will not fight!"
Vain will the purpose prove! thy qualities
Would spur thee to the war. What thou dost shun,
Misled by fair illusions, thou wouldst seek
Against thy will, when the task comes to thee
Waking the promptings in thy nature set.
There lives a Master in the hearts of men
Maketh their deeds, by subtle pulling--strings,
Dance to what tune HE will. With all thy soul
Trust Him, and take Him for thy succour, Prince!
So--only so, Arjuna!--shalt thou gain--

By grace of Him--the uttermost repose,
The Eternal Place!
    Thus hath been opened thee
This Truth of Truths, the Mystery more hid
Than any secret mystery. Meditate!
And--as thou wilt--then act!
    Nay! but once more
Take My last word, My utmost meaning have!
Precious thou art to Me; right well-beloved!
Listen! I tell thee for thy comfort this.
Give Me thy heart! adore Me! serve Me! cling
In faith and love and reverence to Me!
So shalt thou come to Me! I promise true,
For thou art sweet to Me!
    And let go those--
Rites and writ duties! Fly to Me alone!
Make Me thy single refuge! I will free
Thy soul from all its sins! Be of good cheer!
    [Hide, the holy Krishna saith,
This from him that hath no faith,
Him that worships not, nor seeks
Wisdom's teaching when she speaks:
Hide it from all men who mock;
But, wherever, 'mid the flock
Of My lovers, one shall teach
This divinest, wisest, speech--
Teaching in the faith to bring
Truth to them, and offering
Of all honour unto Me--
Unto Brahma cometh he!
Nay, and nowhere shall ye find
Any man of all mankind
Doing dearer deed for Me;

Nor shall any dearer be
In My earth. Yea, furthermore,
Whoso reads this converse o'er,
Held by Us upon the plain,
Pondering piously and fain,
He hath paid Me sacrifice!
(Krishna speaketh in this wise!)
Yea, and whoso, full of faith,
Heareth wisely what it saith,
Heareth meekly,--when he dies,
Surely shall his spirit rise
To those regions where the Blest,
Free of flesh, in joyance rest.]

Hath this been heard by thee, O Indian Prince!
With mind intent? hath all the ignorance--
Which bred thy trouble--vanished, My Arjun?

Arjuna.

Trouble and ignorance are gone! the Light
Hath come unto me, by Thy favour, Lord!
Now am I fixed! my doubt is fled away!
According to Thy word, so will I do!

Sanjaya.

Thus gathered I the gracious speech of Krishna, O my King!
Thus have I told, with heart a-thrill, this wise and wondrous thing
By great Vyasa's learning writ, how Krishna's self made known
The Yoga, being Yoga's Lord. So is the high truth shown!
And aye, when I remember, O Lord my King, again
Arjuna and the God in talk, and all this holy strain,
Great is my gladness: when I muse that splendour, passing speech,
Of Hari, visible and plain, there is no tongue to reach

My marvel and my love and bliss. O Archer-Prince! all hail!
O Krishna, Lord of Yoga! surely there shall not fail
Blessing, and victory, and power, for Thy most mighty sake,
Where this song comes of Arjun, and how with God he spake.

HERE ENDS, WITH CHAPTER XVIII.,
Entitled "Mokshasanyasayog,"
Or "The Book of Religion by Deliverance and Renunciation,"
THE BHAGAVAD-GITA.

[FN#1] Some repetitionary lines are here omitted.

[FN#2] Technical phrases of Vedic religion.

[FN#3] The whole of this passage is highly involved and difficult to render.

[FN#4] I feel convinced sankhyanan and yoginan must be transposed here in sense.

[FN#5] I am doubtful of accuracy here.

[FN#6] A name of the sun.

[FN#7] Without desire of fruit.

[FN#8] That is,"joy and sorrow, success and failure, heat and cold,"&c.

[FN#9] i.e., the body.

[FN#10] The Sanskrit has this play on the double meaning of Atman.

[FN#11] So in original.

[FN#12] Beings of low and devilish nature.

[FN#13] Krishna.

[FN#14] I read here janma, "birth;" not jara,"age"

[FN#15] I have discarded ten lines of Sanskrit text here as an undoubted interpolation by some Vedantist

[FN#16] The Sanskrit poem here rises to an elevation of style and manner which I have endeavoured to mark by change of metre.

[FN#17] Ahinsa.

[FN#18] The nectar of immortality.

[FN#19] Called "The Jap."

[FN#20] The compound form of Sanskrit words.

[FN#21] "Kamalapatraksha"

[FN#22] These are all divine or deified orders of the Hindoo Pantheon.

[FN#23] "Hail to Thee, God of Gods! Be favourable!"

[FN#24] The wind.

[FN#25] "Not peering about,"anapeksha.

[FN#26] The Calcutta edition of the Mahabharata has these three opening lines.

[FN#27] This is the nearest possible version of Kshetrakshetrajnayojnanan yat tajnan matan mama.

[FN#28] I omit two lines of the Sanskrit here, evidently interpolated by some Vedantist.

[FN#29] Wombs.

[FN#30] I do not consider the Sanskrit verses here-which are somewhat freely rendered--"an attack on the authority of the Vedas," with Mr Davies, but a beautiful lyrical episode, a new "Parable of the fig-tree."

[FN#31] I omit a verse here, evidently interpolated.

[FN#32] "Of the Asuras," lit.

[FN#33] I omit the ten concluding shlokas, with Mr Davis.

[FN#34] Rakshasas and Yakshas are unembodied but capricious beings of great power, gifts, and beauty, same times also of benignity.

[FN#35] These are spirits of evil wandering ghosts.

[FN#36] Yatayaman, food which has remained after the watches of the night. In India this would probably "go bad."

[FN#37] I omit the concluding shlokas, as of very doubtful authenticity.